Acres and Acres of

Plowed Ground

Acres and Acres of
Plowed Ground

Bessie L. Anderson

Acres and Acres of
Plowed Ground

Bessie L. Anderson

Copyright © 2001, 2022
Library of Congress Control Number:
TXu 2-319-412
2nd edition – Previously released as:
Plowed Ground
edited, and revised by – Nichele M. Anderson
Copyright © 2001, 2022 All rights reserved

ISBN: 9798351614960

Many thanks to everyone (and I do mean everyone) who helped me bring this across the finish line. Because of your help, I was able to make what my Grandmother could only dream about become a reality. To my grandmother Bessie Lee Anderson whom I called "Grandmo," I wish you were here to see this. I know you would be shedding tears of joy right about now. Thanks for sharing your stories with me about "the good ole' days." Yes they are gone, but they will never be forgotten.

PREFACE

In 1952, Claude Anderson was hired to work for Ford Motor Company. One day a friend told him they were hiring. He went over to the HR office at the assembly plant on old Torrence Avenue that same day. While sitting outside of the office waiting to be seen, one of the foremen walked by. "Hey, what's your name?" he asked. "I need a big guy like you on my team. Come on with me, you can start today." Because Claude was a big man, who stood well over 6 feet tall with a personality to match, he once said, "I fit right in."

Within a few months, he had made enough money to send for his family to come to Chicago. With her 3-year-old daughter Constance, the clothes on their backs, one suitcase, and an old trunk, Bessie Anderson bought a ticket to be on the next train leaving for Chicago. While they were packing her little girl pointed to her baby bottles that were sitting on top of the refrigerator and said, "Baba?" "No, we're going to leave those here," she said. With very little money, but a whole lot of hopes and dreams they arrived in Chicago early the next day.

As fate would have it, and with the additional help from the decision made just a few years earlier by the U.S. Supreme Court in Hansberry v. Lee (Lorraine Hansberry's father), Claude was able to rent a little "kitchenette" apartment just off of Harper Avenue on the Southeast side of Chicago. They were one of only three black families that were "allowed" to move into the neighborhood. After they moved in, Bessie spent a great deal of time cooking, cleaning, and trying to make what she called "….that nasty little hole in the wall" a home. It was during these times, she would sit down and write stories for this book. She once said, her talent for writing was noticed years ago by some white men visiting her school one day when she was just a little girl. But being a colored child in the rural south, her dreams, gifts, and talents never materialized. "I would just sit, look out the window across the fields, and see things in my mind," she said. These "things" she would see culminated into several different short stories. One of them became a completed manuscript she called, Plowed Ground.

Unfortunately, with very little money, knowledge, or encouragement, the manuscript sat in a chest of drawers for years. One day, a neighbor who had moved into the same kitchenette apartment building a few years later, took the handwritten manuscript and typed it up. "It's a good book," she said. "Let me know if you ever get it published." But like the original manuscript, it too sat in the same chest of drawers wrapped in a plastic bag for years.

In 1998 I returned to Chicago after finally graduating from college. During one of the many conversations my grandmother and I would have while she was either preparing a meal, or sitting at the kitchen table; she told me about the book and when she wrote it. The next day, she handed me the typed manuscript of the book. It was in the same plastic bag she had wrapped it in back in the late 1950's.

At that time, I was working as a telemarketer. I decided one day to take the manuscript to work with me. I had planned to read it in between making phone calls to potential customers. At some point, I allowed the automated phone system to "kick in" so I could finish reading the book. I finished it that day. Oh how excited I was to read something which in my opinion needed to be published immediately! But like my grandmother, I knew nothing about how to get a book published, and I had very little money to do so.

As usual after discussing it with a few people, someone told me how to mail a copy of the manuscript to the Library of Congress and have it registered as a copyrighted work. I was also told to mail a completed copy of the manuscript to myself through certified mail.

That way I would have a copy of the book "date stamped" by an official federal agency. Now I don't remember who told me this or why. I found out later this is called, "the poor man's copyright." And although it really doesn't work, and as of today is unnecessary, back then I didn't know any better. So, I did it anyway.

To continue the journey down the unknown, I also re-typed the manuscript making some necessary minor corrections to make the story "flow" a little better. I also typed each chapter in a separate file, saved it onto a now old fashioned "floppy disk," and later on a flash drive. This I thought would make it easier to make changes to individual areas of a chapter if it became necessary. As the years passed, and the trials of life took its toll, I too like my grandmother, lost the motivation to take this further. It was not because of will, but simply a literal lack of knowledge, until now!

I don't know if the story you are about to read is based on reality, some form of it, or completely fictitious, my grandmother never said. What I do know and remember are the numerous stories she told me at the kitchen (or dining room) table over the many meals she prepared all the days of my young life. It is with these memories in mind I have finally finished what she started and share it with you today. I dedicate this book to the memory of Bessie Lee Anderson whom I called "Grandmo," her 3-year-old daughter Constance Anne (my mother), to Claude "Big Andy" Anderson (my grandfather), the clothes they had on their backs, their one suitcase, that old trunk, and the hopes and dreams they brought with them to Chicago in 1952. Grandmo, thanks for remembering and telling me about "the good ole' days." They are gone, but they will never be forgotten.

Your first born,
Nichele

CONTENTS

CHARACTERS

Jim Nutterlow
Plantation Owner
Mildred Nutterlow
Jim Nutterlow's Wife
Their Children
Genelle, Lotis,Terrance,
Patty, Aaron, Bobby
Carrie Johnson
The Nutterlow's Maid
Lucille
Carrie's Friend
Charles M. Moody
Plantation Worker
William Brown
Plantation Worker
Josh Agar
Plantation Owner
Louise Agar
Josh Agar's Wife
Antone LaBlanc
Frenchman in Louisiana
Gee Gee LaBlanc
Antone's Mother
Aunt Magie
Jim Nutterlow's Aunt

PROLOGUE

Big Jim was six feet tall and weighed between two hundred and ten to two hundred and twenty pounds. He had very dark brown wavy hair. He had broad shoulders and blue eyes. If he was riding over the plantation and it was early spring, he always wore riding pants. He wore the kind that blouse on the side with the small legs that fit into his riding boots. If his pants were tan his boots were tan. If the pants were black the boots were black. He wore three-quarter length Chesterfield coats–always with matching shirts and a small tie. Sometimes he wore a bow tie.

In the summer he would wear lightweight pants and of course everything matched. He also wore a ten-gallon hat, spurs on his boots, and he carried a quip. His summer shirts were made of a Pongee material. They were white with the lacey look in the front. The long sleeve shirts had a flair cuff on the end. He also wore arm gathers, and frock tailcoats. Big Jim smoked a pipe which made him look even more handsome. He wore a solid gold wedding band, and a solid gold watch in his watch pocket with a gold chain attached to it. He even had one tooth with a gold tip on it. The gold watch belonged to his father, and his father's father before that and so on. Big Jim wore a size ten shoe. Jim Nutterlow was thirty-one years old. He was a wealthy plantation owner, tall, dark, handsome, and a very exciting man.

Mildred Nutterlow had fox red hair, and green eyes. She stood about five feet one or two inches tall. She weighed about a hundred and twenty five pounds with a very small waistline. Carrie (their maid) always told her she had a waist like bird legs.

Her dresses were frilly and worn over dozens and dozens of petticoats. After six babies Mildred still weighed the same. She was always very careful about her waistline and her lovely face. She washed her face with cow's milk every morning, and she would pat it dry with a soft wash cloth. She had lovely olive skin, no moles, marks, or blemishes on it—just sheer beauty.

She wore a size five and a half shoe. All of her shoes had pointed toes with small heels. Some were satin, and some buttoned on the side. When the lace-up shoes came out she had those too. Later came the low top to the ankle shoes and then the below the ankle shoes. Of course she had them all, and they all matched both the dresses she wore and her bonnets.

When she walked her petticoats rustled. Everyone took a second look when Mildred Nutterlow walked by. She always carried a matching drawstring bag lined with satin. In the summer, she carried a Japanese fan that she would use to cover her mouth with while she looked over it. She wore gloves the year round and carried a handkerchief all the time. She had a beautiful smile, lovely teeth, and long eyelashes too. Mildred Nutterlow was twenty-five years old, a very lovely woman.

Josh Agar was fifty-one when he married Louise Ivy. Josh was a short man, not too fat, with a small bald spot just starting to show on top of his head. He had sandy hair, and blue eyes. In the summer, he wore white suits, with white shoes, a hard-straw hat, and a small black bow tie all the time. Josh also had a potbelly, not too pot though—just enough. He danced real well and he was always oh so sweet with the ladies. He smoked cigars, and he also sported a gold watch with a gold chain hanging from it. In the winter he wore the Chesterfield coats of all kinds and colors. He had pants suits of all kinds and colors too. No matter the season, Josh was well dressed at all times.

Like Jim Nutterlow, Josh owned land. But Josh also owned a paper mill in Carolina, a lumber camp up in the northern part of Tennessee, and some more land there too. His plantation in Centerville adjoined Jim Nutterlow's. His house sat back off the road. The house had Elm trees and Magnolia trees sitting in the front yard, with lovely flowers, boxwood hedges, and a large fig tree near the back fence going into the garden. They had plenty of servants, but none of them stayed close to the house. They would come and work during the day and go home at night. That's the way his wife Louise wanted it. Josh came to Centerville from Atlanta but his people before him were from out East–Boston.

Josh was always busy trying to make a living for Louise. Although he had plenty of money, he never thought about anything else. He was always busy making more money–that's all. Even though she was younger than him, Josh really did love his wife Louise. He always told her how sweet, soft, and pretty she was. He always bragged to everyone about his sweet, young, pretty wife. When Louise would go out with him, he loved to show her off as Mrs. Josh Agar.

Louise was thirty-five when she married Josh Agar. She had large brown eyes and brown hair–not dark brown though. Like Mildred Nutterlow, Louise was pretty, but she kept her hair cut short with a "v" shape in the back. Her hair was naturally wavy.

She had cream-colored skin, and a few moles at the nape of her neck. She also had a brown splotch on her neck. Some people call these birthmarks, but it was pretty. She was taller than Mildred Nutterlow. She stood about five feet five or six. She weighed about a hundred and thirty-five pounds and she wore a size six and a half shoe. She was Louise Ivy before she married Josh Agar. She came to Centerville from Baton Rouge. She had two sisters. Both of them were married by the time they turned thirty-five as well. That's the way it was in the Ivy home. The girls had to be married by the age of thirty-five. That's why Louise married Josh as soon as she turned thirty-five. She knew she didn't love him but she knew how Mr. and Mrs. Ivy felt about their girls getting married.

Her parents were gone all the time. Her mother–Carlotta Ivy, was from England and they spent almost all of their time over there. Her father's name was Lowell Ivy. They owned a large plantation just outside of Baton Rouge called the Ivy Plantation.

Chapter 1

Jim Nutterlow met Mildred at a county fair. She was all dressed up in her Southern Belle dress made of flowered silk over almost a dozen petticoats. He smiled at her, and she smiled back at him. Jim owned a large plantation his father had left him. He brought bulls, and sows with him to sell at the County Fair. It was one of those days when everyone showed up for the County Fair, the old and the young. Mildred was standing by the canned fruit stand just looking pretty to draw a crowd. All the pretty girls stood by the stands to draw the crowds. The fair lasted five days. By the time the fair was over, Jim had sold his steers, his sows, and made a hit with Mildred. By mid-August they married and spent a few days in New Orleans. On their last day there, they rode the ferry down the river. Later that night they left for home.

Because this would be a new home for Mildred, Carrie went down to the meadow and cut wild flowers. She had the house all cleaned for the coming of Big Jim's new wife. Big Jim's plantation was very large, with plenty of horses, cows, hogs, and land for miles to farm. For a while, everything was just so wonderful.

Not too long after this, the first Nutterlow baby was born–a girl. There was a big celebration. Other plantation owners came from all over. The next Nutterlow kids came in very quiet without all the big fuss they made over the first one. Carrie stayed with the Nutterlows almost all the time when the kids were small. During this time, Mildred was going back and forth to New Orleans to get clothes for the kids.

On one of these trips she met Antone LaBlanc. Mildred was happy again. Antone was different. He was always clean, and he didn't smell of horses all the time like Jim did. She would go back to the plantation thinking only of Antone. Oh sure, she made out like she was a real happy wife and mother. But deep down inside, her heart was with Antone. Mildred had found her longtime lover again.

Jim worked the field hands hard. He had a wife and kids now and he never let up. One day Mildred thought, "I've been home a long time now. I'll see if Jim will agree for me to go to New Orleans for a while." She went into the kitchen. "Carrie!" "Yessum Missie!" "I'm going to New Orleans in a few days, I think. I'll plan everything tonight. You wash up my lightweight things and iron them so everything will be ready." "Yessum Missie," she replied. Mildred left for New Orleans on Friday. She told Jim she was going to see her relatives. Carrie had to take care of the house, the kids, cook, wash, iron and go to the fields part time. But with Mrs. Nutterlow being gone, she doesn't have to put in that part time work in the field. She had to see after the children now.

Carrie also cooked for the field hands. They're the ones that come to Mr. Low and work around the barn. They feed the chickens, pigs, clean out the hog lot, and milk the cows. By the time they get through it's almost dark. They have a long table out in the yard under a big black gum tree, with two lanterns at each end of the table. They eat out there because Mr. Low doesn't allow blacks in the house—not the men. He thinks they might assault Mrs. Low or something.

They eat their greens, peas with okra, garden fresh tomatoes, English peas out of the garden, green sweet peppers, potatoes, and fresh garden lettuce with the curly leaves. They also eat some kind of pudding and plenty of buttermilk that has been kept cool by putting it down in the cellar. They eat all of this; and when the boys get through, Carrie comes out and gets up all the cans, plates, and the long bread pan. Their glasses are the large Snow King baking powder cans. She takes the boy's things to the wash shed where she washes the clothes every week. She washes their dishes in the big iron pot where she boils the clothes because she didn't dare wash them in the kitchen where she washes Mrs. Low's dishes. "The Boys" as they are called, are different ages–35, 40, 45, and so on. But to Mr. Low, they are still boys. He considers them his special Niggers.

Soon, it's time for Carrie to pull out the large wooden tub and the two new tin tubs. Mrs. Low would always tell her friends how she got the wooden tub long before the Titanic sank. She hated to get rid of it. After Carrie bathes the Nutterlow's smaller kids, she puts Davis Talcum Powder on them, their nighties, and nightshirts. In the summer, the boys wear nightshirts too. The cloth is made of some kind of soft material like Pongee that Mrs. Nutterlow bought in New Orleans. The girls wear long soft frilly nightdresses with ruffled tails and small belts. "Hop in bed children. I's got to empty dis bath water," Carrie said. She empties all the water and gets an old Crocker sack that's used for a mop to get the water up that was wasted on the floor. One of the kids cry out, "Hurry up Carrie so you can tell us all about slavery time." They giggle when Carrie tells them her tall stories about slavery and how high a slave woman could jump in a barrel when they lived over the river on another plantation. After this, Carrie brings in snacks for them to eat.

They have shortening bread, milk, and water out of the well. While Carrie is talking, they all go off to sleep. Carrie gets up and gets the mosquito nets out to put up over the bed for the Low kids. Then she picks up all their clothes, and fixes up the room real neat. Mrs. Low likes for their rooms to be neat after they have gone to bed.

Mr. Low comes into the kitchen for another snack. Carrie fixes it and gets his bath water ready. While he bathes, Carrie waits out on the back porch. After he's finished she empties his water and wipes up the floor. He puts on his sleeping clothes and goes up into the parlor. Carrie calls out to Mr. Nutterlow, "I'm through. I'm going home now." "All right Carrie," said Mr. Low.

Carrie goes home down the road. She starts singing, "Old Satan is mad and I'm glad, dun got over at last. He missed dat soul he thought he had, dun got over at last." The echo rings over the cotton and the cornfields. The pigs give out a grunt. The chickens in the hen house also say something when they hear Carrie's songs. Even the stars twinkle when they hear her sing. Some nights when it's very dark, Carrie sings a little louder to keep the evil spirits away. They only come out on dark nights. But tonight, the moon is very shiny and looks so soft up there. No evil spirits tonight, just the insects in the weeds, the frogs in the pond, and every once in a while a cow will let out with a, "Moo."

She finally gets home and gets herself ready for bed. She makes a big fire out in the yard around the wash pot and fills it with water. While the water heats, she sweeps and cleans up her shanty. Then she goes to the spring for some cooling water. She comes back and gets ready to bathe herself up some. She uses an old tub. Because it has a hole in one side, she props that side up real high. Then she bathes and dries off. When she gets through all she has to do is set the tub outdoors. The water has leaked out of the tub down through the cracks in the floor that are as wide as your hand.

She gets out her nighties made of Calico or some other sack. Sometimes, Mrs. Low brings her some bundles of cloth from New Orleans. She makes a dress, a petticoat, drawers and a gown all out of the same bundle of cloth. Almost all the time it's bright red or golden yellow. She powders up with her Sweet Pea powder and gets her mosquito net out. It's an old one Mrs. Low gave her when she bought new ones. It has as many holes in it as a fish net, but Carrie gets under it just the same.

Later that evening in the still of the night, Carrie hears a soft sound at the door. At first she thinks she is dreaming, but then she hears it again. She gets up. "Who's dat out dare?" "It's me Carrie." "Oh my goodness Mr. Nutterlow. Dem chillin dun got sick. I knowed they were eating too much of dat shortening bread and pudding. I told dem they was eating too much. I's git my dress on Mr. Nutterlow." "No Carrie! I came to see you and to see if you were all right." "Me Mr. Nutterlow? Why I's jest fine." "Here, I brought you something." "For me?" "Yes, go on and drink it." Carrie turns the can up and drinks it. Then she giggles. "Hey, hey, dat tastes like dat we had at Christmas." "It is Carrie." "It show makes you feel good." "Yes Carrie it does," said Mr. Low. After all the small talk, Carrie puts out the lantern and goes back to bed. Mr. Low left just before daybreak. "You get up to the house early in the morning Carrie." "Yes Sir Mr. Low."

Chapter 2

By daybreak, Carrie gets up and gets ready to go. She starts singing a song as she goes on up the road. The roosters are crowing, and across the fields you can see a light mist in the air. Some of it is smoke from the pot Billy the handy man started. He has already made a fire in the stove, and put the coffee water on. Carrie comes in and fixes coffee for everyone. Then, she starts making breakfast.

She makes hot grits with pan sausage or middlin' meat, either hot cakes or hot biscuits, and a pitcher of milk for the kids. But before this is served, Carrie brings in the water and towels for the face washing. They all wash up in those lovely white bowls that have a pitcher and a wash basin to match. They both sit on the wash stand next to the towels that hang off the wall on a rod next to the wash stand. It is a beautiful old-fashioned set that has been handed down in the family for years.

After breakfast is served the Nutterlow children get dressed for the day. Some go horseback riding. Some go down to the brook in the meadow. Some just sit out in the yard under the magnolia trees. Mr. Low has already been out riding over his plantation finding work for the field hands to do. The field hands ate their breakfast out under the same gum tree in the yard. They had hominy grits, middlin' meat, coffee, biscuits with molasses or canned preserves, and milk. Just as Carrie comes out to take up their pans and plates to the wash pot for washing, the bell rings. Everyone knows that means it's time to go to the field. They all get in the wagon and head for the field singing or whistling, "Way down yonder."

After Carrie washes all the dishes, she starts to clean the house.

She goes out in the garden and gathers the vegetables, and out to the smokehouse to get ham or shoulder meat for dinner. While she fixes dinner, she cleans some more. By now it's close to noon, and the kids start showing up wanting cold water from the well. Carrie goes out and gets it for them. "You chillin wash up now cause it will be time for dat bell to ring soon." Because it's a nice day, Carrie fixes the table in the hall. It's cool out there.

By the time she finishes the bell rings, and Mr. Nutterlow rides up. By this time of day, he has been to the village store and over to his neighbor's plantation. When he gets off his horse, he simply turns it loose. There is always someone there to put the horses up when the Nutterlow's get through with them. When he walks in, the children greet Mr. Low with the usual, "Hi daddy!" "Hello children," he replies. He washes up and sits down to eat. "I got a letter from mother today. She will be home Saturday." They all rejoiced, "Mother will be home!" She has been gone a month now.

After they all finished lunch, some took a nap. Some planned to go catch tadpoles later. Some of them went swimming in the pond. Carrie sounds off, "Don't you chillin go to fer." All together they reply, "Yes Carrie!"

Mr. Low leaves too. He walks down to the path that goes down to the bayou. Every day around this time, Louise Agar strolls down this way . She likes to pick wild flowers, and Mr. Low likes to help her pick them. They spend the afternoon there until about four o'clock or so. They have a nice hideout just in back of the bayou. Mr. Low has been sweet on her ever since she came to town from Baton Rouge. The Agar's live on the plantation adjoining the Nutterlows.

On Saturday morning everyone was up early to meet Mrs. Low at the train station. Everyone dressed in their Sunday best. They left early because the train from New Orleans gets into town about eleven o'clock. They shop while they wait for the train. Mrs. Low washes her face on the train because she cried almost all the way home. She hated to leave Antone. He was her childhood sweetheart but he has been in Europe for years going to school. His mother took him back to Europe when she first heard about the romance between him and Mildred. She felt that Mrs. Low wasn't good enough for her son. He got married once, but his mother broke up the marriage. She thought Antone was too young. Antone was a true Momma's Boy. He went everywhere with her—Europe, South America, and everywhere in between.

His father—Etto LaBlanc, went down with the Titanic. Before they moved to the U.S., they lived in France. Mr. LaBlanc gained his fortune from selling imported silk and Pongee material from France that was used to make ladies clothes. He had just purchased some new material to sell in the U.S. when the Titanic went down. Both Etto LaBlanc and all of his materials were insured. Trust funds had been set up for Mrs. LaBlanc and Antone long before this happened. Mrs. LaBlanc's first name was Gee Gee. After Mr. LaBlanc died, she became the sole owner of the business.

Mildred came from a nice family. They lived in and around New Orleans all of their lives. Her father—Frank Dullerwee, was an engineer. He finished school in England and came over to help build roads, bridges, and canals all over the United States. He settled down around New Orleans. Her mother—Millie LaAgue, was a French girl who met and married Frank Dullerwee during one of her visits to the states. She was a smart, charming girl who was always very well dressed. Her father was a painter in France, a very successful one too. To keep her mind off of missing Antone, Mildred thought about all of these things, and the wonderful childhood she had.

Soon, the train pulled into the station. The children yelled,

"Here's the train. Oh! There's mother!" They all rushed up to her and hugged Mrs. Low. Everyone put on a good show. Mrs. Low was so happy she cried. But deep down inside she was crying about Antone. The kids were sincere though.

After eating a bite at Joe's Place, they all got ready to go home. "Oh mother, I have a pretty dress I made while you were gone," said one of the children. The other Low children sound off, "I made a feather fan while you were gone." "And I made a birdhouse in the Elm tree mother." "I have a jar full of tadpoles." "I made a flower bed mommy." What she really meant was she made a weed bed.

As usual, Carrie was back home busy fixing things up. She went down in the meadow and picked Honeysuckles. They made the house smell beautiful. As soon as the wagon pulled up, the kids started calling, "Carrie here's mommy!" "Lord a mercy, you show been gone a long time Missie. I show is glad you dun come home. I cooked your favorite, loganberry pie." "Thank you Carrie," Mrs. Low replied. "I picked the berries down in the meadow." "How has everyone been Carrie?" "Everybody is been jest fine Miss Mildred. I unpack your things now Missie." "Alright Carrie," Mildred replied. Carrie starts to unpack. "My my Missie, you show got some pretty clothes. So soft and smell so pretty. Dat show must be a pretty place, dat New Orleans." "Oh yes Carrie, it's a beautiful place."

Carrie opens the case with her jewels, rings, and pictures in it. She dropped a picture. "Oh Missie, is dis your brother's picture?" "No Carrie!" It was a picture of Antone but Mrs. Low does not dare tell Carrie this. "Put it under that vase over there Carrie!" "Oh Missie, with a pretty picture like dis, I'd let it stay out so everybody could see it." "No Carrie!" She yelled. "Don't ever show this picture–ever! Remember that Carrie!" "Oh, no Missie, if you don't want nobody to see it." "Bring me some cold water Carrie!" "Yessum Missie."

28

While Carrie goes to get the water, she re-hides the picture. Then Mr. Low comes in for a minute. "Oh hello darling! I'm tired. I think I'll rest now," she said. "Alright Mildred, I'll see you tonight." "All right darling," she replied. Jim was already late to meet his neighbor's wife. When he got there she was all hot and mad. She had even been asleep. He tried to explain to Louise that Mildred came home, and they all went to meet her at the train station. "I don't care if King Louis came home. You be here tomorrow Jim Nutterlow and I mean it!"

Later on, Mrs. Low wakes up and gets dressed for dinner. "Gee mother, you look pretty," said one of the Low children. Mr. Low came in and washed up because he smelled like perfume. Mildred wears Jade. She would know it wasn't her perfume on him. Because dinner was special tonight, Carrie wore her dress up apron. She made two spoon bread puddings, baked hen with dressing, baked shoulder, small green peas, greens with cornbread dumplings, garden fresh lettuce with the curly leaves at the ends, small tomatoes cooked, and made into gravy. There was also corn on the cob, shredded cabbage, and carrots. Carrie made a few egg pies, and some of her best biscuits too.

All during dinner, the Low family talked about everything. All the kids had something to tell their mother. The oldest girl–Genelle, talked about her friend who went to Big Springs, Texas to visit and how the family over the river went to North Carolina for the summer. "Oh mommy, I want to go someplace," she said. "O.k., you can go to Natchez to see Nelia," Mrs. Low replied. "Oh, goodie!" One by one, the rest of the kids sound off, "Mommy can I go someplace too? I want to go someplace. Oh boy, me too!" Ms. Low always promised the kids they could go someplace but she would never let them go. Maybe this time she will.

It would give her more time to rest, and to think about Antone.

It was a hot night. Mildred complained about how they needed electric fans in the house. "In New Orleans they have fans in the ceiling and this keeps the house cool," she said. Big Jim didn't say much. He knew Mildred always complains after a trip to New Orleans. After a while he was asleep. Mildred sat by the window and looked at the stars. Antone was in her heart. A little while later, she went into the parlor and slept on the couch. She thinks about Antone as she falls asleep. "Oh Antone, how I miss you my love. How I need you tonight."

Chapter 3

The crowing of the rooster the next morning awakens everyone. Then they all turn over because they know it is not quite time to get up yet. After another quick doze, the chirp of the birds, the crickets in the grass, the hens cackling in the hen house, the little baby chicks crying, 'peep, peep,' and all kinds of other sounds from the barnyard; everyone knows, now it's time to get up.

Carrie is walking down the road singing the song she always sings. When she arrives she gets breakfast ready, and starts the usual bringing in of the water for the face washing. The Missum is home so Carrie sets the table out in the hall. It's cool out there. The children talk on and on about what they are going to do on their trip. Carrie comes in with the Luzianne coffee. Mrs. Low tells Carrie to wash up the children's things. "I'm going to let them take a trip for a few weeks." "Yessum Missie," Carrie replied.

All day long Carrie washed and fixed meals. Mr. Low was out overseeing the field. At lunchtime, Mildred tells Jim she wanted to go into the village just for the afternoon. One of the house workers fetched a horse, hitched it to the buggy, and had it all ready and waiting for Mrs. Low. Mildred gets all dressed in the new dress she bought in New Orleans. She puts on her perfume, her jewelry, and gets ready to leave. "You be careful Missie," called Carrie. "All right Carrie," she replied. She was real happy because she's gonna call Antone and talk with him.

There are only two phones in town, one at Mr. Henry's store, and one at the courthouse. Everyone uses that one. But the phone in Mr. Henry's store is the only really private phone, and he always steps outside whenever a lady wants to use it.

Mildred used it to call Antone. Luckily, his mother was out of town. Antone had just got up from taking a nap. Mildred talked with her Antone and cried. "Cee Cee my love, don't cry," he said. "Antone when will I see you?" "Now now, you'll be coming back to New Orleans again soon," he said. "I love you Antone. Don't you love me?" "Oh yes! Yes!" he replied. Antone always sounded so sweet to Mildred. She loved his voice.

Uncle Henry walked back in just as Mildred hung up the phone. "Oh, I guess no one is home this time of day," said Mildred. "Yessum," Uncle Henry replied as he tipped his hat. "You look pretty this hot day Mrs. Low." "Thank you Uncle Henry," she said as she switches out of the store.

Mildred walks around town to show off her pretty clothes and to look at the different things they had in the store windows. Other Southern Bells pass by and give her that jealous look. Mildred's hair is fox red and she has green eyes. They accuse her of buying dye in New Orleans and dying it, but they were wrong. It was naturally red. It makes no difference to Mildred what they think. Southern Bells are jealous of each other and that's that. "Is that Jim Nutterlow's wife?" "Yes," one of the girls replied. "I hear she spends almost all her time in New Orleans." They whisper some more and switch on up the plank walk. Mildred bought some hair combs and ribbons for the girls, and a few other things for the boys to take with them.

At last the kids are going on a trip. They thought the week went by slowly. They all got up early Saturday morning and got ready to go to the train station. They were there in plenty of time for the train. They all hugged Mildred goodbye as the train pulled up. "Oh Mommy, thank you for letting us go. Goodbye Daddy, tell Carrie goodbye." They all waved goodbye.

Jim and Mildred stayed around for a while, but Jim was in a hurry to get back. He told her he wanted to go over to the North Range today, because tomorrow he had to go to the flat land. The flat land was miles and miles of leveled farmland. As far as the eye could see, it was nothing but black bottom land. "Planting was late this season because of the rain," he said. "All right, I'll ride out there with you when we get back," she said. "Oh no my dear! It's too hot and the horse flies are bad when it's hot like this. They will bite you and make red sores. I want you to stay pretty." It wasn't hard to convince her not to go. Mildred wanted to preserve her beauty for Antone anyway. The real reason he didn't want Mildred to go along was because he had to be down by the bayou at four o'clock to meet his neighbor's wife. He knew if he was late she would be mad, very mad.

Back at the plantation Carrie had cleaned, washed some, scrubbed some, and cut fresh flowers from the meadow. She had a big fuss with one of the workers because she won't let him come down to see her sometime. "Maybe I will let you come. I don't know yet thoe," Carrie said. After Carrie served all the supper, she got ready to go home.

She was still thinking about her big fuss with one of the workers. When she got home she cleans up her shanty singing as she always does. After everything was finished, she just sat there on her porch in the dark. The frogs were crooking in the pond. The insects were singing their songs in the weeds. In the night every once in a while you hear a "whippoorwill." All through the night the birds let out with a "chirp, chirp."

Soon, Carrie goes to bed. Late that night she hears a tap on the door. "Whose dat out there?" Mr. Low hadn't been to see about Carrie in a long time. "Mr. Low aughten you be up dare at the house with the Missum?" "Awe Carrie, you know why I'm here." After a while he leaves.

The next morning Carrie is up and in the kitchen on time. Mrs. Low was sleeping late. Carrie sits on the back porch waiting, thinking, and looking at the blue mist as it rolls up into the air. After a while, Mrs. Low calls out, "Carrie!" "Yesum," she replies as she goes into the house. "Good gracious a live Missum. You sleep out here all night?" "Yes Carrie it's so hot at night and Mr. Low sleeps so bad and restless at night." "When it gets cold you will catch your death out here," Carrie said. Carrie starts to put everything together in her mind. She thinks, "She don't sleep with Mr. Low at all." Carrie understands a few things; and soon, she'll understand a lot more.

Chapter 4

Jim Nutterlow goes into the village and gets the mail. Mildred Nutterlow gets a letter. It's addressed from Marie Antone, but she knew it was from her Antone. They planned it this way. "I'm longing for you my dear. You must come to New Orleans if not but for a few days. I love you. I need you. Love yours always, Antone." Later, Jim comes in. She tells him that Marie's niece is getting married. They want her to help with the wedding plans. They get up early the next day. They get to the station in plenty of time. When the train pulled up she cried. "Darling I hate going like this." "Nonsense, go on honey. It's not the end of the world." "You know I'll hurry back to you I promise." She was so happy because she would be seeing her Antone tonight.

Antone's mother had gone for a few days to visit some friends. Mildred and Antone went everywhere together, Baton Rouge, Shreveport. Those few days turned into weeks. But one day on their trip, one of the Nutterlow kids got sick. Mr. Low had to go pick him up. He called Mrs. Low at Marie Antone's house. That's where she said she would be. The maid answered the phone. She knew what to say if anyone called for Mildred Nutterlow. She took the message. When Antone and Mildred returned at 4:00 a.m. she gave them the message.

The train left at 7:30. "Oh Antone," she cried. "Why now?" "Now, now, we will be together again soon." Antone took Mildred to the train. She cried all the way there. Their good-byes were sloppy; but somehow, they got through it. On the train ride home, she thought over the days and nights she spent in Antone's arms. Now she had to leave him.

"I knew I should not have let those kids go off by themselves. I should have kept them at home. Why didn't I!" she said as she pounded her fist into her hand.

Mr. Low met her at the station. She hugged him and seemed so worried. He assured her there was no need for great concern. "The kid ate too many fresh berries while hiking through the woods with his friend. Then they came upon a spring and he drank too much water. He got really hot and had stomach cramps." "Is that all?" Mildred asked angrily. "Well that's enough. He could have cramped to death," Jim replied. "Yes what I mean Jim is, it's not too serious thank God. I was so worried all the way home." "If I had been able to talk to you I would have told you this. Mildred, where were you that time of night?" Jim asked. "Oh Jim, we went to a shower. We waited late because it was so hot. Marie got loads of gifts," she replied. Then she turned her head and looked into the face of her Antone. Jim glanced at Mildred, then he looked to the left into the face of Louise. He gave a signal to the horses, "Yah, getty up there!" Jim and Mildred rode home together side-by-side, but miles apart.

Carrie greeted Mildred, "Welcome back Missie." "Thank you Carrie," she replied. While she pulled his hair back away from his face she said, "How is mommy's boy?" "Oh I'm o.k. Mommy, I'm sorry I got sick." "That's alright," she replied.

Jim rushed right out. "I'll see you later Mildred." "O.k. Jim," she replied. He knew he had to get to Louise. He had not seen her in a few days. But she knew he had to go get the kid. He would be seeing her today though. She would be there, so very soft and smelling so fresh. They ate and slept down by the bayou in their favorite hide away. It's so nice and quiet there.

Louise has been telling Jim she can't go on meeting him like a cheap sporting woman. "What do you want me to do Louise?"

asked Jim. "Do you love me Jim or do you love Mildred?" "Do I have to tell you over and over again Louise? I've loved you from the first day you came here from Baton Rouge. I wanted to take you in my arms and kiss you. All I could think of was how I would feel with your body next to mine. But you were already married to Josh Agar, and he's my next-door neighbor. Oh, I knew his body was next to yours every night. But I wanted you Louise, I still do. How can you think of my needs as a flirtation?" "Oh Jim! Take me, hold me, do what you like. I need you too."

After they kiss she says, "I knew Josh was too old for me, but by the time you are 35 in my family, you have to get married. I had never had a man before and I thought this was the best ever. Josh was so kind and gentle. But Jim, when I'm with you, you make me feel like I was just being born again. I think about you when Josh touches me. I pretend it's you. I have to because he expects something of me sometimes. The same as you do of Mildred." Louise, Mildred and I haven't slept together in ages." "Oh come now Jim!" Louise replied. "With six kids you must sleep with her some time." "Well yes, when we first got married. But Mildred decided after the last baby was born, she wasn't going to sleep with me anymore. She said she was tired of being all stuck out like a field hand. She wanted to keep her beauty, and she wasn't going to have any more babies." "Oh Jim, I hope I get one of your babies soon. Then you'll have to be mine." He kisses her again. Then he says, "It's getting late. Let's go Louise." "Now Jim, don't rush me." "Oh you she devil, kiss me." Jim and Louise fold into each other's arms and kiss until they are breathless. "I love you." "I love you too. Goodbye darling, see you tomorrow."

When Jim gets home, he sees Carrie sitting on the back porch. "Is Mrs. Nutterlow asleep Carrie?" "No Sir, she went to visit a neighbor." "What neighbor?" "I don't know. The neighbor over in the hallow I guess." "What are you doing Carrie?" "I'm making Chaw Chaw." "What were you and Willie fussing about down by the millstream last week?" "He jes want to come a courtin me sometimes." "Did you tell him no!" "I don't know if I did or not Mr. Low." "Well you don't want anybody there with you at night. You are my woman. All plantation owners have an extra woman. I know you know better than to tell anybody, don't you Carrie?" "Well if you say so." "I can't get along without you Carrie." "Alright," she said. Jim pinches Carrie on the butt. She grins, "O.k. Mr. Low." Jim walks outside to see about his son. He was out sitting under a shade tree playing with a knife.

Mildred came home. "Where did you go Mildred?" Jim asked. "Oh, I went to see Louise Agar. She wasn't home so I went over the hallow to visit some." Jim stood silent for a minute trying not to look shocked.

Carrie served supper early because houseguests were coming over tonight. They all like to sit around drinking apple cider and joking about how pretty each other's wives look. The men sneak in a wink or two at them as well. They play the old gramophone to the tunes of, "Old Susanna," and "Let Me Call You Sweetheart." They play a lot of the old songs from years past, and some of the new ones too. While the music is playing, they waltz with each other's wives. At around midnight, the men do a bit of extra squeezing of the lady's hands. Everyone goes home very cheerful because they all got to flirt with each other and make eyes at one another.

The rest of the Nutterlow kids will be home soon. This was a nice rest for them and Mrs. Low. She had plenty of time to sit around and think about her Antone. "Gee, how I miss you Antone." She also thinks back about the guest they had over for supper.

Louise Agar sure did look at me funny," she thought. "But Josh was his usual old self, real sweet with all the ladies."

A few days later, all of the Nutterlow kids arrive home. "Oh Mommy! We had a wonderful time. Please can we go again?' they all cry out. "Oh yes, yes next summer," replied Mrs. Low. "I show did miss you youngins," Carrie said. "We missed you too Carrie, but we had a good time."

The Nutterlow kids range in age from Genell who is 16, Lotis who is 15, Terrance who's 12, and Pattie who's 10. Then there is Aaron who's 9 years old, and Bobby who's 7. All at once they try to tell their mother everything they did during their trip to Natchez. Mildred raised her voice a little and said, "Now you can all talk, but one at a time so I can hear you." All through breakfast, the Nutterlow children go on and on talking about what they plan to do next summer. Mildred looked at Aaron, the one who got sick and said, "Now don't you eat too many berries and get sick again Aaron." "O.k. mommy," he replied." She looked away while the kids kept on talking about the trip.

Mr. Low gets up to go. "Oh must you go now darling?" said Mildred. Jim said, "Yes, you can't run a plantation at home." "I know," answered Mildred. "But I wanted to talk with you." "We can talk tonight. I have to go now," said Jim. "I suppose it can wait," she replied. Mildred thinks it over and realizes it was too soon to ask Jim to go back to New Orleans, but she's getting restless and she knows Antone is too. She must see him before the summer ends. The kids will be in school and she won't be able to see him as often like in the summer months. She thinks, "I'll wait and make up some excuse."

Chapter 5

The next day was hot. Mildred thinks, "Gee, I wish I was in New Orleans." Jim Low came home from the plantation early. He rarely came home early. He and Louise Agar had a fuss. He was late again, but he had to see about some land he plans to buy. He realizes that when he gives Mildred up, he will have to have enough money because she will sue for all it's worth. He knows he doesn't have as much money as Josh Agar, and Louise will have to be supported in style. Jim tried to explain all of this to Louise but she told him, all she wanted was his body next to hers day and night. "I want a baby Jim, one of your babies. I don't want any old wrinkled baby by Josh. You've got to give me one of yours Jim." They fussed about this all the time lately.

Josh Agar is gone almost all the time. He runs a plantation down in the lower lands called, "The Delta Land." And from time to time he goes to check on things at the mill he owns in Carolina. This leaves Louise Agar with plenty of time on her hands. She is getting tired of meeting Jim Low down by the bayou. She wants him to come over to her house and sleep with her the nights Josh is away. They fuss about this too a lot lately.

Mildred Nutterlow was taking a nap when Jim came in. She awakes, "Oh, hello darling. How did it go today?" "All right I guess," Jim says in a short voice. "It will be cool soon now with fall coming, will you take me over the plantation?" Mildred asked. "Yes, later," said Jim scratching his head.

Carrie serves supper early because she is going over to Lucile's house tonight. Lucile lives on another plantation. "They gonna have prayer meeting.," Carrie told Mrs. Low. "The meeting starts soon."

"All right Carrie," she replied. Carrie gets through and leaves singing and thinking if Willie will be there tonight. Carrie cleans up her shanty and gets ready to go. A buggy and a wagon full come to get her.

Carrie gets on the wagon and they all head for Lucille's house for prayer meeting. They all greet one another. Things are very holy like because Tract Meeting is getting ready to start. Willie was there. He looked at Carrie and she looked at him. Willie decided right then he was going to take her home tonight after prayer meeting, and she was gonna tell him something. Carrie fooled him though. She stayed all night with Lucile. Willie hung around, but no luck. Everyone went home full of the spirit. Willie walked on down through the pass on by Carrie's house. He looked over at Carrie's house and thought, "One of these days I'm gonna be hiding in there somewhere when Carrie comes home, and scare the hell out of her. She tries to be smart." He walked on down the road grumbling to himself.

The next day, there wasn't too much going on around the Nutterlow house. It was a partly cloudy, partly fair day. It rained over the river this morning. It rained about in other places. Carrie was busy all day cooking, cleaning, canning, and thinking about Willie. She thought about how he kept looking at her last night at the prayer meeting. "I wonder what he was thinking about." Then she starts to sing. She went through the day as usual and went home.

Saturday morning the Low family went into the village to spend the day. Carrie got through with everything and went home. "The preacher will be here for a month and I got to clean house cause he'll eat dinner with me one day." She starts singing, "Down By The River Side." She cleans, scrubs, and sweeps the yard. Lucile came over and then she and Lucile got ready to go to the village.

Lucile's husband works around the general store. He cleans up and sweeps. Carrie goes there almost every Saturday. They stay until the store closes. Almost all the plantation workers meet up at the general store on Saturdays. They drink beer that's in a barrel sitting on a prop with sawdust sprinkled on the floor in front of the barrel. They eat oil sausage, cheese and crackers, sardines and State Plant cookies. They really have a good time down in the "Quarters," as they call it.

It's Saturday night, and about the last fling for a while before the big meeting starts on Sunday. "We won't be able to do much but, "Pray to God," one of the women said.

By midnight everyone was getting ready to go home. A lot of jokes were told around the store tonight, and a lot of men were flirting with the gals. Some of the men were standing out in the shadows drinking white corn whiskey out of a stone jug. The creek goes by the store and some of the men were down by the creek drinking and shooting craps by lantern light. In some of the thick bushes you hear someone let out with, "Stop! You're hurting me." Everything goes on Saturday nights.

Then someone said, "Let's go home. The store will be closed after a while." They all come up, get in their buggies and wagons, and head for home. They're all laughing and talking about the fun they had tonight. Someone on one of the wagons had a banjo, and strums the old banjo to the tune of, "Down Yonder." Some tell jokes, some try to sing, and they all laugh the night away. You can hear the train whistle blow, the echoes ringing out, the dogs barking, the insects moving in the weeds, and the birds are chirping in the trees. "Ha! Ha! Ha! Laud a mercy. I show did have a good time wid yall tonight Lucile." "O.k. Carrie," said Lucile. "I git off here and go down through the peanut patch to the house." "All right Carrie. We'll see you tomorrow."

Carrie starts humming. She gets to her shanty and unlocks the door. She lights the lantern and starts to pull off her Calico dress when she hears, "Hello Carrie." "OOO Willie! What, what , what in the world you doing here? You scared me." "I decided it was time I toned you down Carrie. I know you don't like me, but you don't know if I can or can't. You have to let me prove to you I can." "You get out of here William Brown right now and I mean it before I holler and call…" "Call who Carrie?" "I'll call Mr. Jim." "Yes I know." He puts the lantern out and holds Carrie so tight she can't holler. She can hardly breathe. After a long struggle, Carrie gives in. "I'm yo man now Carrie, and you's my woman." Willie left right at the peep of day.

Carrie gets up early, but she didn't have to go to the Nutterlow house this morning. They stayed in the village and went to a show. The kind of show they were showing in and around 1919. They will spend the day with Jim's Aunt Maggie. She's his rich Aunt.

Her wealth is from Confederate money that she still has. She still remembers how rich her people were before the Yankees came. Rather, that's what Aunt Maggie says. The Nutterlow kids get a kick out of Aunt Maggie's tall stories. She's been telling them for as long as they could remember. Her wealth now though was from rented land. She had plenty of that and some money in the bank. She even sold some of the land in Adams County.

Aunt Maggie always talked about when she lived in Atlanta. She still had an old trunk filled with a lot of old lace, and other old things she had before the war. The only difference was sometimes Aunt Maggie would say she had those things before the Yankees came. Then she would say before Lord Cornwallis came past their house one day. All of this is real confusing to the Nutterlow's 7-year-old. He doesn't know Cornwallis from a stone wall. Half asleep he asks,

44

"Who are the Cornwallis?" This makes Aunt Maggie start telling her stories all over again. By the time she finishes this time, they all are almost asleep.

They like to go to Aunt Maggie's because she lets them roam through her things and she cooks real good goodies for them. She still has a lot of silks and satins they wore in Aunt Maggie's day. Mildred likes to listen to her too. Jim was always restless, but he made out.

On Sunday morning, Carrie goes to church. Everybody from miles around goes to Mt. Pleasant Baptist church for Tract Meeting. The log-built church sits in the midst of some Cedar trees. "Hello Sister, Hello Brother," are the greetings given during the hand-shaking. This goes on for two to three hours or more. As soon everyone goes into the church, the singing and praying begins. After a while, the preacher comes out and starts preaching. He preaches for about two hours and the Sisters start to shout.

He tells them, "There's a big devil chained down thar," as he points to the floor. "And he don't want to go down thar." They all shout, "Amen!" Then they jump up and shout some more. Some try to hold down the ones that's shouting. Then they start shouting all over again. It goes on like this all day until about 4:00 or 5:00 in the evening. When they get through, they spread dinner on the ground. They have make-shift tables, but it's called, "spreading dinner on the ground."

They all eat and talk about how good the preacher preached, and how they were all full of the spirit. Everyone exchanged food and had an old-fashioned good time. It was just like the tent meetings on the old campground. Soon, night begins to set in. Because there's not enough lanterns to go around to have preaching at night, everyone gets ready to go home.

They all get into their wagons and buggies and leave.

All the way home they talk about how good they felt and how good the preacher preached. The preacher went home with Brother and Mrs. Noah Johnson. They are truly husband and wife. They got married in Monroe County. Willie rides home with Carrie. He holds her hand in the wagon, pinches her, and sneaks a kiss every once in a while. He feels on Carrie's hips too. Everyone says good night as they leave the wagon. Willie kisses Carrie good night but he doubles back through the cabbage patch right into Carrie's back yard.

He knocks, she opens the door, and in comes Willie. Carrie says jokingly, "You ought to have gone on home Willie. Aint you full of the spirit?" "Uh, uh," said Willie. "That's why I'm here. You know you wanted me to come back cause you gave me a jerk when you got off the wagon." "I did dat?" Carrie says. "Yea, you did," said Willie. Willie takes Carrie in his arms and kisses her. While they were both still filled with the spirit, Willie puts out the lantern light. It seems that everyone was full of the spirit that night.

With the Tract Meeting going on and all, everyone gets up early the next day. They had worked hard all year for this month. They got all their demanding work done. They go about the small work and everything else they have to do so they can get through. Some leave for church as soon as they are finished. They go in singing, praying, shouting. And as soon as church is over, they head for the field. Some went to the kitchen. Some went to the wash pots. Some went quilting and other different things. All kinds of things went on during the Tract Meeting which lasts for about a month.

During this time, some of the plantation workers go to the meetings every day. Some go just on certain days. And of course, the new converts were sure to get their religion. On the last day of the meeting, they went all over town and borrowed lanterns so they could have the meeting that night. It was a big night. They paid the preacher by taking up a collection for him.

This is the preacher's big night too. He preached a real strong sermon that night. They took up $20.00 in the collection plate for him, and gave him all kinds of other stuff too. There was molasses, canned fruit, and all the meat he could eat like hog meat. The preacher really had a load full. He shakes hands with as many as he can before breaking up time. Then they all get into their wagons and buggies and head for home.

During the church service, Willie sat where he could look right at Carrie. He took her home in his wagon, just the two of them. They had a good time laughing and talking. Willie stayed all night. They slept late the next day.

Moody and Willie are good friends. He is the main field hand that works around the barn. He came by and woke them up. "My goodness! I shoulda been up and had dem grits on cooking." Carrie gets up, rushes into her clothes, and gets on down the road to the Nutterlow's house. It was too late for Willie to take his wagon home, so he let his mules graze around Carrie's house. He left the wagon there for the day.

Jim Nutterlow rode by later that day on his way to different parts of his plantation. He saw Willie's wagon. He asked Moody if that was Willie's wagon. "Yes sir Mr. Jim," said Moody. Jim Nutterlow had told Carrie he didn't want anybody there with her a long time ago. Moody said, "Old Willie been sweet on Carrie fer a long time Mr. Jim. I guess dae plan to go to the preacher man pretty soon." Jim Low doesn't say anything.

Carrie gets through as early as she can. All day she hummed and thought. When she was finished she called out to the Nutterlows, "I's through and fixing to go home now." "Good night,"

47

said Mrs. Low and the kids. Jim didn't say anything.

When Carrie got home, Willie's wagon was gone. The door was locked, and the key stuck in the chimney. "Um, I wonder where is Willie." Then she thinks, "That no good hobo. He was gon take me to the preacher man and marry me. He just wanted to sleep here with me. That no good rascal."

Carrie cleans up her shanty, takes her bath in her leaky tub, and goes to bed. She had just got off to sleep when she heard a very hard rap at the door. She thinks it's Willie. She got up and flung open the door because she's mad at him a little. "You, oh Mr. Jim. I thought….." "Yes I know Carrie. You thought I was Willie. Willie had to go over to the North Range for a while." "Why dats in Monroe County," says Carrie. "Yes I know," says Jim Low. "I told you Carrie not too long ago, I didn't want anybody here with you at night Carrie!" He slapped her, "Didn't I Carrie!" "Yes Sir," she cried. He slapped her again. "But Mr. Jim I got to have me a man of my own too." "I'm your man Carrie and you are not to have another one. Next time I won't be this easy with you!" He left long before daybreak.

Carrie gets up early. She goes to the kitchen but she wasn't happy though. She thinks about Willie. "He won't be back for a whole month from the North range." She thinks, "I don't know what I'm gon do but I've got to do something. Maybe I'll run away with Willie. I sho do like him."

Jim Low went down to Carrie's every night for a week to take care of her needs. Louise Agar had gone up to Tennessee with Josh for a while. Jim tells Carrie she will have to give up the idea of marrying Willie and that his father kept Laura all the time. She was his woman. "And besides Carrie, I need you. I don't have a woman. My wife don't sleep with me. Come on Carrie promise me it won't happen again." "All right Mr. Jim, I promise." Carrie wasn't happy about the promise though. "What will become of dis? Willie might get some kind of notion about me and Oh me! That would be awful." Carrie thinks as she cleans the Low's house. She's in a deep study. She didn't hum none today.

Chapter 6

The next day Mildred Nutterlow gets a letter from Antone. It's addressed, "From Marie Antone." Marie or Sherie were the nicknames Antone called Mildred. It said, "Marie, I must see you at once. I have the need for a woman. You must come to me soon. Mother went to Waco to see friends. Please come at once!"

At breakfast the next morning Mildred says to Jim, "Don't you think I should go get the children's clothes for winter? The new shipment will be in on the riverboat and I want to get some things before they pick all over them." "Yes you go Mildred. I've got to go up to the North range. We are putting in some new fencing up there. I won't be home every day. Carrie can stay here and see after the kids." "Oh Jim, you never can go with me any time," she replied. Deep down, she knew she didn't want him to go with her. As she packed to go she was thinking, "Thanks a million Jim! Antone I'll be there soon my love." Jim Low took Mildred to the train the next morning. Mildred hugged Jim lightly as if she hated to go, but she was real happy inside. She would be seeing Antone again. She waved goodbye from the train window to Jim.

Louise Agar came home the very next day. Josh had to go out to Carolina, to see about some timber. He would be there a week. That was fine with Jim. Now he won't have to meet Louise in the woods. He slept there every night with Louise and she was real happy. This was what she wanted, Jim's body next to hers. Jim went to the house and the plantation every day but left early so he could get to Louise early.

Louise was sweet but Jim was in a deep study. Louise noticed he wasn't himself. He kept thinking about Carrie. Jim made the best of this night. Josh Agar will be home tomorrow. Jim kissed Louise. He left late that night and promised to meet Louise down by the bayou as they kissed goodbye.

Jim slept a little late the next morning. Carrie was sitting on the steps when Jim came out. "Where are the kids?" Carrie looked up, "Oh, some went one place, and some went another. They'll be home for lunch." "What did you do last night Carrie?" "I didn't do nothing. I went home, cleaned up, took me a bath, and came on back here." "Was Willie here yesterday?" "Yes sir. He came by to tell me he was sorry he had to leave and go up on the North range without telling me that day. He said you sent him up there. Then him and Moody went out to where they were hauling hay." Jim pulls Carrie up to him and kisses her, "O.k. Carrie, I love you." "Mr. Jim you can't." "Oh yes I can, and I do. I'm going to shave now. Fix me some hot water Carrie. And fix me some hot cakes." She fixes the hot cakes and hums to herself. She feels real special. She's Mr. Nutterlow's sweetheart.

She wonders what Willie would say or Mrs. Nutterlow. Louise Agar would really blow a fuse if she knew about this. But Carrie doesn't know about her and she doesn't know about Carrie. Yes, Big Jim Nutterlow seems to have everything; a wife, a mistress, a Negro woman, six beautiful children, a large plantation, and plenty of money. On top of all of this, Jim doesn't know that Louise Agar is expecting a baby–his baby. This is what she said she always wanted.

One day, Jim got a postcard from Mildred. It said she would be home soon, and she had a big-time shopping with her cousin. She did shop for two days, but the rest of the time was spent with Antone. When Antone took Mildred to the train station, what a coincidence, Gee Gee LaBlanc–Antone's mother was there. She got off the train at the same time. They had a big run in.

Gee Gee told Mildred she had better not see her with Antone again. If so, she would expose her to the public. Mildred threatened her too. "Expose what may I ask?" "I don't know yet but I will find something!" Gee Gee slapped Mildred's face and called her a hussy. Mildred cried. What a sad ending after such a lovely time with Antone.

Mildred cried almost all the way home. Jim was there to meet her when the train arrived. She hugged him tight and cried. Jim told her, "Honey next time I'm going with you. You always cry when you come home." He took her in his arms. "Oh Jim, I love you." "Hush now, come on let's go home." Deep down Mildred was mad and sick over Antone's mother. They got home and took all the things in. "Gee honey, you must have bought the whole riverboat," Jim said. Mildred smiled.

Soon, the kids started wandering in. They went through those things like mad. Mildred was tired. She bathed and went to bed. Jim stayed around the house tonight. He wanted to talk to Mildred. She got up about dark and ate. The kids got ready for bed. Mildred sat in the parlor in the dark. Jim bathed and got ready for bed. He went into the bedroom to talk to Mildred, but she was out in the parlor. Jim went out there, and they talked. She complained about the heat. Jim didn't say much. He was used to Mildred complaining when she first comes home from New Orleans. Jim took her in his arms. She tried to pull away, but Jim was a big strong man, 6ft tall, about 200 pounds or more. Jim loved Mildred, and this was their night. But all she thought about was Antone. This was unusual for Jim and Mildred, because they hadn't slept together in ages.

The next day, Mildered was worried. She decided a long time ago she didn't want any more Nutterlow babies. She was wondering if she had got another one. "Gee," she thought. "I hope not."

When Jim came home for lunch, and they were alone she asked Jim, "Were you drinking last night Jim?" "No," he said. "Why?" he asked. "Oh nothing," Mildred replied. They talked for a while about the neighbors. Then Jim got up and rushed out to meet Louise. She would be mad if he was late. He met her but she wasn't feeling so well. "What's the matter Louise?" Jim asked. "Oh Jim, I don't know." "You better see a doctor; maybe it's the heat." "Yes, I plan to," she said. Jim just kissed her and they left. "I'm going to see the doctor tomorrow." "All right, but let me know some way how you are Louise." "O.k. Jim," she said.

That night the Nutterlow kids talked on and on about their new clothes. Everyone was real excited. Carrie got through with all the dishes. She was going home early, because she was going off tonight. She got home and got cleaned up for her trip.

Willie came by and they left. They went over to the old cotton house. They stayed there late and fussed. Willie asked her, "I can't understand why we always fussing Carrie?" Carrie stood up and told him, "I wanna go to the preacher man Willie Brown and you ain't said nothing about taking me! I think it's bout time, don't you?" "All right, don't get so mad Carrie. I'm gon take you to the preacher man." "Oh yea, when?" "Well Carrie, I got to get some money first." "Let's go Willie, I'm tired!" "O.k. Carrie, remember I'm gon take you to the General Store Saturday night and bring you home." "Well, we'll see Willie," she said.

At home while she was cleaning up her shanty, Carrie started to worry. She was in for it now because the last time she and Willie were together, Jim Low sent him up to the North Range, slapped her around, and made her promise she wouldn't see anyone again. Carrie was worried, real worried. "What I'm gon do now?" she thought. Carrie didn't hum none tonight.

Back at the plantation, Big Jim was worried too—not about Carrie, but about Louise. Three days had passed and he had not heard from her. The next day he rode by that way. Josh was doing some paperwork on the porch, they spoke. Jim got off his horse, walked up, and propped his foot up on the porch. With one foot on the porch, and his other foot on the ground he said, "How's everyone Josh?" "Oh, all right I guess. Louise went to Baton Rouge for a while. She was sick when she left. She kept throwing up. I told her to go see a doctor." "Oh Yea?" "Yea, she'll be back Friday. I heard from her yesterday." Jim stayed a while then he left. He was all right now. He knew when Louise would be home. Jim thinks back, "Throwing up? Mildred threw up when she was having the kids. Gee, I wonder if Louise is having a baby, my baby! That's all she talked and fussed about lately. It can't be though."

Jim got home and stayed around the house all evening. Mildred came out. They talked for a while. He told her he saw Josh and that Louise was in Baton Rouge. Mildred said, "Gee, I wish I was on a trip." "Oh come now Mildred! You just came home honey. I'm going into the village tomorrow. You want to go?" "Yes Jim, all right," Mildred said.

The next day, Jim and Mildred were up early and got ready to go into the village. Mildred dressed in a pretty dress. Everyone took a second look at Mildred Nutterlow when she walked down the plank walk in the village. She was very beautiful. Jim liked this. He could see the envy in the other men's eyes. Jim bought some things for the plantation. Mildred just went along to show off her pretty dress. She did buy some gifts for the kids.

While Jim was down at the Blacksmith's shop, Mildred went over to the only private phone in the village. As usual, Uncle Henry went out while she made her call. She called New Orleans.

Antone was home. As luck would have it, he answered the phone. She talked with him. He told her he wasn't for sure, but he thinks he's going to Europe. His mother suggested it. "Oh, Antone, for how long?" "I don't know Sherrie. Now please don't cry. I will try to see you or let you know something." "Please do Antone, please." "Ok now, I have to go. Jim is with me today. Goodbye Antone." "Goodbye Sherrie." Mildred was so weak and nervous when she left. She was just sick. Jim met up with her. They ate at Joe's place, and then got ready to go home. All the way home, Mildred was quiet. Jim talked and talked. Mildred answered with a "yes" or "no" every once in a while. But she was thinking about Antone.

After they got home, she told Jim she wanted to rest for a while. "O.k. Mildred, I'll be back soon." "All right Jim," Mildred answered very weakly. All she was thinking about was that Antone was leaving. Then she thought about his mother and their run in. She thinks, "I hate that woman! I could scratch her eyes out! Someday I will." Then she falls asleep.

Jim goes down by the bayou just in case, but no Louise. He thinks, "Gee, Louise must be real sick. I wonder if she is really going to have a baby. Is it really my baby?" Jim gets home and gets washed up for supper. Carrie was real quiet today. She just worked straight on through. She was thinking about Willie all day wondering why lately, they fussed all the time when they were together. She likes Willie alright enough, but she just wonders.

Mildred got up from her nap and tried to make the best of it. The one thing that stuck out in her mind was Gee Gee LaBlanc was taking Antone away from her. She had heard about how she always managed to break up all of Antone's romances with other girls, even his wife. Mildred asked for the tomatoes on the table. Someone passed her the tomatoes. After they finished supper, she walked out onto the porch and then into the yard. The workers spoke to her as she walked about looking at the flowers and trees. She told one of the helpers she wanted him to take up the dead leaves from under the magnolia tree tomorrow. "Yes Ma'am Missy," he replied.

Jim came out afterwards and sat on the steps. They talked about different things. A few minutes later Moody came riding up. He spoke to them and they spoke back. Jim asked him where he had been. "I went to take the wagon wheels to be fixed." "Oh yes," Jim replied. Then Jim walked out to the barn. Moody unhitched the wagon while they talked. Moody said, "Oh! Mr. Jim, I saw Mr. Agar in the village." "Yes Moody," Jim replied. "Yes Sir! He told Mr. Henry he was going to Baton Rouge. He said his wife was real sick over thar." Jim just said, "Yea." "Yes Sir!" Moody said. Moody finished with the horses and walked over to the house with Jim. Carrie had left his dinner on the table in the yard covered with cloth.

Now Jim was upset. He wanted so much to see Louise and talk with her. He tried to think up an excuse to go to Baton Rouge. Jim worked on this idea in his head for a while until finally, it worked out. Genelle was ready to go off to school and Jim told Mildred he would take Genelle to her school and stop off at a few auctions on the way back. Mildred said, "Good grief Jim! You have plenty of cattle now." "But you never can tell when you will run into a good buy honey." "All right Jim, I'll be lonely for you," Mildred said. "You get some rest Mildred, you look tired. I'll be back before you know it honey."

Chapter 7

Everyone in the Nutterlow house helped Genelle pack to go away to school. The next day, she and Jim left to catch the train. Moody went along to bring the buggy back. They waved goodbye to Moody as the train pulled off. "Did they get off all right Moody?" Carrie asked when he returned. "Uh, huh," Moody answered. Then he thinks about how sad Mr. Jim looked when he told him what Mr. Agar said about his wife, but he didn't say anything.

Carrie finally gets through washing, and starts cooking supper. She went out to the clothesline to pick up something that fell on the ground. She asked Moody when he had seen Willie. "Not since Saturday night at the General Store," he said. "If you see him tonight, tell him I say come down to my house and I mean tonight!" "All right Carrie, I'll tell him."

Moody left early after Carrie got through with supper. Carrie left too. She had to clean up her shanty because she knew Moody would get Willie the word. She hummed, cleaned, got out her leaky tub, and took a bath. When she finished, she set the tub out in the yard. As usual, all the water had leaked out down through the cracks in the floor to the ground. Carrie hummed a lot tonight.

She was feeling real good. She got dressed in her Sunday best and sat on the porch listening to the sounds of the night. Far off in the distance, she heard horses. "One is Willie's I know, and the other one is Moody's." The horse's footsteps got louder. Carrie starts to hum, "Tenting tonight, tenting tonight, tenting on the old camp ground." She sings and fans. It's one of those hot September nights with a pretty harvest moon just peeking out of the sky that's filled with stars. Carrie looks up at the stars. After a while they rode up and unmounted. "Hello boys," Carrie called out. "Hello Carrie," they answered as they came in and started talking. "Where you been all week Willie?" "I been bailing hay, we finished today." "Yeah?" "Yeah, Mr. Jim gone to take Genelle to school. They went on the train today," said Moody. "Is Miss Mildred home?" Carrie asked. "Uh huh," Moody replied. "It's a wonder," said Carrie. Moody went up to the other end of the porch and went to sleep on a pallet.

Carrie and Willie talked and talked, but Willie didn't talk about what Carrie wanted to hear. She wanted to hear him talk about taking her to the preacher man. He was telling her what a big time they had when he was on the North Range. He talked about how they went over to a buddy's house over on the Monroe County side and he had a whiskey still. "They really whooped it up!" Willie said. "Willie, was thar any women thar?" Carrie asked. "Not out in the woods. But we went to the store one Saturday thar in Monroe County day sho got some good looking gals thar," Willie said. Carrie gets mad a little. Willie tells Carrie. "The riverboat will be through here pretty soon." "What! The Riverboat Show! Hot diggedy dog!" Carrie said. "When, next month?" "Uh huh," he replied. "How you know Willie?" "I saw the paper they put out all painted up." "Hot Dog! I'm going boy!" said Carrie.

School has started, and all of the other Nutterlow kids were back in school. Big Jim was away too. This gave Mildred plenty of time to think about Antone. Late that hot September, Mildred got a letter from Paris. It was dated around the first week in September. "My goodness, this was right after I talked with Antone. That woman took him away after all. Oh Antone, you promised to let me know. Why didn't you? Why? Oh why? I love you so Antone."

She looks at his picture, pressed it to her heart, and cried. Then,

Carrie walks in. "What's the matter Missum?" she asked. "Oh Carrie, I'm so lonely and unhappy." "Oh honey, Mr. Jim will be back soon." "I know Carrie," if that was only it. Mildred covers up her face with a small pillow stuffed with soft feathers and covered in pink satin. She thinks, "No one knows how sad and lonely I am, and it's not for Jim." While Mildred wept and wept Carrie thinks, "Gee, she's real lonely for Mr. Jim. But he don't be lonely like that when she's away. He never says anything much when she's gone."

Jim took Genelle to school and stayed with her until she was settled in, then he left. "Bye honey, I have to stop off at a couple of auctions on the way back." "O.k. Daddy, give my love to everyone." Jim didn't stop off anywhere until he got to Baton Rouge. He asked someone how he could get to the Ivy Plantation. It was the plantation Louise's family owned–her childhood home. Jim borrowed a horse from the living stable and went out there. Louise had just returned from the doctor. Josh had gone to Atlanta on business. While Louise was lying in bed, the maid brought her a Mint Julep. She felt so much better now.

A few minutes later Jim arrived and called out, "Louise!" "I recognize the voice," she said to herself. "Jim! Oh Jim! Come in!" Jim dismounted his horse and came in. Louise rushed into his arms. "Oh Jim, how on earth did you find me?" "It was easy. Everyone knows the Ivy Plantation." "Oh Jim, Josh will be back tomorrow." "That's all right, I'm leaving tonight. Oh! It's so good to see you." They went for a walk. Jim hugged Louise until she was almost breathless.

"When will you be home Louise?" "In about a week Jim." "Boy that will be good. I heard you would be here all the fall." "Oh no, Josh wanted me to stay awhile. I was so sick for a while, Jim." "Yes, I know." "I'm better now though." "When is the baby due Louise?" "Next April, the doctor said." "Oh Louise, you she devil." He kissed her again. They walked back to the house. Jim mounted his horse and waved to Louise. She waved back as Jim rode off. He was a very handsome man, very tall with broad shoulders. Louise thinks, "Gee, if only he was all mine right now."

Jim spent the night in Baton Rouge. The auction was the next day. Jim bought an Angus Bull, three sows, and a stud horse. Jim rode home very happy. Louise will be home soon. The train ride home was slow to him. It pulled into the station the next morning. Moody and one of the other helpers met Jim because of the stock he brought home. "There's Mr. Jim!" said Moody. They rushed up to him. Jim greeted the boys. He gave them some cigars. He bought presents for the whole Nutterlow clan.

Back at home, Carrie was busy as usual. Everyone went out to meet Jim, but Carrie kept on peeling the peaches she was canning. Jim came through the house, "Hidy Carrie!" "Morning Mr. Jim." Carrie had heard the gossip about Big Jim saying he was taking Genelle to school, but really going to see Louise Agar. And she was still mad with him for sending Willie to the North Range that other time. "He want all the women, but the women can't have no man," Carrie thinks while she was canning and cooking her dinner. She served dinner early, cleaned up everything, and went home. "I'm gon fix that Jim Nutterlow tonight," she says to herself. She met Moody in the hallow and he took her to Willie's place. Carrie stayed all night with Willie. He was going to take her to the preacher man for sure now, as soon as settlement time came.

Carrie thought, "Maybe Willie might take me this time." She left real happy this time. They didn't fuss none. As she rode home with Moody she said, "You know Moody, I really like old Willie." "Yes, and he's stuck on you too Carrie," said Moody. Carrie giggles.

When she gets home she gets ready to go to work. She gets there, puts the coffee water on, and started fixing the other breakfast. Jim Low came in. "Good morning Carrie." "Morning Mr. Jim." "Where did you go last night? And don't tell me you didn't go nowhere because I was down there off and on all night and you weren't in there sleeping. So, I want to know where in the hell did you go Carrie?" "Oh, I went over to Lucile's and after it got so late I stayed all night." "Who was there?" "Oh, nobody but Lucile and her husband. Lucile got her baby brother over thar for a while." "All right Carrie, but you be home tonight when I come down there." "Yes Sir Mr. Jim," Carrie replied.

Chapter 8

The next day, Jim rode into the village to see Mr. Scott about his sorghum mill. It was time to make molasses. "Howdy Mr. Scott! I need a mill," said Jim. Mr. Scott tells him he can borrow one next week. "Jim, have the boys strip and cut the sorghum this week," said Mr. Scott.

It didn't take long for the word to get around that the men will be making sorghum next week on the Nutterlow plantation. People come from miles around to the sorghum mill at night. Men, women, plantation helpers, and others come because everything goes on at the sorghum mill. The women bring baskets of good food like fried chicken, and other good things to eat. If a certain man eats out of someone's basket they'll say, "She's sweet on him." The men bring a jug or two of corn whiskey they made, and there's always a banjo player. They have a big time at the sorghum mill. The men make up barrels of molasses for their bosses. They meet up every night and go from plantation to plantation until all the sorghum is made up into molasses.

By now it's mid-November. The fields have already turned brown. Almost all the cotton has been picked. All the corn stalks have been gathered. The potatoes and peanuts were dug and plowed up. The collard greens have been replanted for winter. The last summer crop of tomatoes were picked, and all the cotton stalks have been knocked down, and cut up to rot. This will make the ground rich soil for next year. Fertilizer has been scattered all over the farmland, except the bottomland.

Big Jim left early Tuesday morning. Genelle will be home for Thanksgiving. He went to meet her at the train station.

Carrie had been busy cooking plum pudding and all kinds of different cakes and pies. Genelle brought a friend girl home with her from school. The girl's parents were in Europe most of the time. They spent the winter there. She was one of those poor little rich girls that was left behind at boarding school and was very lonely. Because of this, Genelle invited her home for Thanksgiving.

The house was all cleaned for the girl's visit and smelling good with all the good things Carrie was cooking. One by one Genelle introduced the girl to everyone in the family. "And finally," she said, "This is Carrie. She's our mommy when mother is away. She's our everything." With a great big smile Genelle's friend said, "Hello Carrie!" "Hidy Missum!" Carrie replied. "Mother we ate on the train. I want to take her for a ride before we eat supper." "Alright Genelle," said Mildred. Moody brings the horses around and the girls go for a long ride. "Oh Genelle! I just love it here!" the girl said.

The oldest Nutterlow boy right away had a crush on Genelle's friend, but she was too old for him. Almost every young boy has fallen madly in love with an older girl once in a lifetime. He fussed with Genelle for teasing him and making him look silly. They all had a good laugh.

Mildred Nutterlow was a real mother while Genelle's friend was there. She took them into the Village to a show, and gave them a real old-fashioned plantation party. All the nice young plantation boys around the same age as Genelle came to see her friend from boarding school. They talked about school and the different plays they put on at school. The young men talked about how fast their horses could run. One boy was in Texas and got to see a rodeo. He talked about how those Texas boys could rope and ride.

The party was over by midnight. Southern parties go on quite late. Everyone bids one another good night, get into their buggies, and go home. The Southern boys are very nice and gentle with their Southern Bells. They help them get into the buggies first then spread a blanket over their laps. Then they climb in. And of course along the way they hug and kiss. There is also a Lovers Lane not too far up the road. It was a short road only used by the helpers when they take cotton to the cotton house. After a party, you would find plenty of buggy tracks there.

Finally! The ShowBoat comes to town. Everyone has been looking forward to this since September. The Nutterlow's go in and spend the night with Aunt Maggie so the kids can see the show.

During the first weeks the ShowBoat is in town, all the white people go. They have the first two weeks. The next two weeks are for the colored, the Indians, and the few Chinese people living in the town. They all have a big time. Carrie goes every night because she and Willie are pretty tight now. When she wants to see him, she goes over to his house and comes back before it's too late. She just knows he is going to take her to the preacher man now.

After a month, the River Boat Show closes. The last night on their way home, everyone is happy and gay. They all laugh and talk about how those gals could dance. One man talked about how he saw one gal's pretty pink silk bloomers when she hiked up her dress. One laughed and said, "When that one on the end kicked up her leg, hot dog! Man that was a good show."

The usual things happen whenever a show comes to town. Some of the boys leave with the show and some of the women too. Willie said, "Did you know old Bo Bo went wit the show and Miss Mattie's girl did too? Dae going to work wit the show." "Yea," said another. "Dae git way off from home and git down sick and can't come home like dem other gals did." "I don't know what dae do," Willie said. "But I do know Miss Mattie got money for her son dat got killed thar during da war." "Yea, I heard bout dat too," someone said.

From now on, the banjo player had him some new songs to play until the next River Boat Show comes to town. He played his new tunes on the wagon ride all the way home. They all laugh and make merry. They had a good time while the River Boat Show was there.

Chapter 9

All last year, Jim and Mildred talked about buying a car. But Jim never got around to doing anything about it. Mildred was tired of the buggy. Even though their buggy was real fancy with a fringe around the top of it, she wanted them to have a car. She was secretly hoping Jim would finally decide to buy one. That way, whenever she came home from one of her shopping sprees in New Orleans, the family could meet her at the train in their new car. But when Mildred first spoke about them buying a car, Jim said, "Nonsense!" Then he remembered when he visited his cousin, and how much fun it was driving. He thought about it almost all night. A few days later, Jim told Mildred he thinks he might go over to Atlanta and see about a car soon. "Oh Jim! You don't mean it!" "Yes honey," he replied.

Jim left at the end of the week. He was gone for two days. When he returned, they all kept very quiet about it. The car was to be delivered in ten days. They waited and counted the days. On that Saturday morning everyone was up early. They ate and got dressed in their Sunday best. The train got in from New Orleans about 11:00. They shopped while they waited for the train.

Somehow, everyone from miles around had heard that Jim Low had ordered a car–a Model T from Atlanta, and it was coming on the next train. It was a big day. They all went into the village to see Big Jim's new car. It was like a fair when the train rolled up. Dogs were barking. The horses bucked, some even ran away. Then somebody hollered, "There's Jim Low's car!" Everyone gathered around to see it. Some blew the horn. Others just looked at it. Some put their hands on the wheels. Some were wondering if Jim could actually drive a car. But he really could drive. He learned how when he went to visit a cousin up in Tennessee back in 1914, and he still remembered how. A lot of the people up there had Model T's. Sometimes Jim wished his land was up in Tennessee.

After cranking it up, Jim got in the car. He had to get this over soon to show everyone he really could drive. He drove around the dirt road and back. Then the other fellows wanted him to show them how to drive. He took turns showing different ones how to drive. Some just did miss a tree or two, or the side of a store.

But after almost all day of telling everyone where he got it, they all were going to get them one too. One of the kids came over and told Big Jim that mother said she was tired and wanted to go home. They all piled into the car, and got ready to go home. The kids looked over the car all the way home. It was real big and they were the first plantation owners to buy a car. The boys thought their daddy was about the biggest man east of the Mississippi River. Moody came along with them to bring the buggy back. It truly was a great day. For the next six months, this was the talk of the town–Jim Nutterlow's Model T.

The next day Jim showed Moody how to drive his car. They both knew he would have to drive it some because Jim was a very busy man. It took about two or three hours but finally, Moody had learned how to drive a car. After he took some bark off of a few trees and crushed some bushes, he finally got it. Moody left late that night because the time spent learning how to drive made him the last to get through with his work. He whistled all the way home thinking about how he could drive a car. He was so happy, he walked three miles to tell Willie about it. Willie was over at a friend's house next door. At first, they didn't want to believe it. But after a while, Moody finally got them to believe him.

After they shoot a few craps, they all left to go home. They only had twenty cents between them, but each one won some money. One would win it awhile, then the other. They talked about Jim's car until they all got to their own shanty's. Moody couldn't think of anything else all night but that he could drive a car. There was little sleeping for Moody that night.

The fields were ready for harvest now. And the helpers were busy gathering the harvest–the corn, the cotton, and everything else. The sorghum had already been made. The potatoes had been dug up. The peanuts had been pulled, dried out, and sacked. Even the Low children had picked pecans along the river. The Black Walnuts had been picked up and put out to dry. Later on, the plantation helpers will hull them. Carrie had canned all kinds of different things, even the Watermelon rinds.

Christmas time would soon be here. Mildred went to New Orleans to buy Christmas goodies for the whole family. Jim drove her to the village to catch the train. "This is more like it," Mildred thought. She kissed him goodbye. "I'll be back in two days," Mildred told Jim. He just nodded because Mildred always stayed longer. But this would be the saddest trip Mildred Nutterlow ever made to New Orleans, because Antone was gone to France. Mildred thinks as she goes about shopping, "Oh Antone, how I need thee my love."

Although she was sad, she managed to buy all the things she came for, even the gifts for the plantation helpers, Carrie, and everyone else. She ate at the same place her and Antone ate so many times before. On the third day the last day she was there, she cried.

When she arrived at the train station in Centerville, Jim Low wasn't there to meet her. Moody had to go into the village to get some wire for fencing. Like everybody does, he was just wasting time around the village waiting until the train came in. Whenever the train pulls into the station, everyone stands around and looks at the train to see who gets off and who gets on. Moody looked and there was Miss Mildred. "Oh, dares Miss Mildred," he said. Moody went up and spoke to her. "Oh Moody, where is Jim?" "I don't know Miss Mildred. I came down here for fencing wire. I was getting ready to head back in jest a few."

She sent Moody up the track to the baggage car to get the things she had bought. He loaded it all on the wagon. With Moody's help, Mildred climbed up on the wagon, and they started out for the house. Mildred was mad of course, but she made the best of it. Just as they got to the pathway leading to the house, Jim rode out. Moody stopped the team. "My goodness Mildred, what are you doing on that wagon?" Mildred looked around and asked Jim, "What on earth were you doing coming from back there?" Jim stuttered for a minute and said, "I was looking for a stray calf." Mildred angrily replied, "I told you I would be back in three days!" "Oh Mildred you never come back on time." "Well this time I did!"

Little did Jim know that Antone was gone to France. And little did Mildred know that Jim had been to the secret hideout where he and Louise Agar would meet. As she opened the door Carrie said, "Laudy Miss Mildred, we didn't know you was coming back dis soon." "Jim knew I'd be back Carrie!" "O.k. Mildred, you always say one day and it's two or three days later or a week. Let's skip it Mildred, you've rode on a wagon before!" "Did I say I didn't Jim? All right!" She yelled as she threw down her hairbrush. "Take it easy Mildred. Why don't you go upstairs and take a nap." Mildred went to their room and cried. She was upset, not because of the wagon ride, but because she wouldn't be seeing her Antone soon.

Chapter 10

The nights began to get cooler. Jack Frost started nipping at everyone's noses. The Nutterlow kids were getting home later because the days were getting shorter. Carrie and Moody hid all the gifts in the attic. But they don't call it an attic. The kids called it the trunk room because all the old trunks are up there, along with the spiders and cobwebs too. They clean it out once a year around June or so, and look through all of the old pictures. But this time of the year, no one goes up there.

One day, one of the Low boys came home with a picture he drew at school. "Look mommy, a pretty Christmas tree!" "Yes, yes dear. I want you boys to go down by the river and cut me some holly, gather some mistletoe, and bring in some ivy too," Mildred said. "All right mommy," they replied. Everyone is thinking about Christmas. The children change their minds about what they want almost every day. Carrie is busy cooking and planning the Christmas meals because different people come in at Christmas time. Carrie thinks, "I'll be cooking for days." Carrie starts gathering all of her old spices. She put up her pumpkins for her pies long before Thanksgiving. She put two or three in the loft in the barn in some cotton seeds. She also put up four or five Watermelons in meal at the end of the summer. Carrie always does this. She also canned Opossum meat so she could have it for their Christmas feast. She's singing today. She is very happy.

It's a Saturday and the boys are gone to hunt for chestnuts and huckleberries. The girls are busy getting their gifts wrapped. Mildred and Jim went to the village. It will soon be Christmas day. Every once in a while, a shot rings out because somebody is hunting today.

Carrie thinks, "My I like this time of year." Mildred buys more gifts while she and Jim were in the village. They pick up the mail too.

There are lots of letters from different relatives and friends. Some will be there, some wishing them a Merry Christmas. She and Jim got back home early. Jim goes down to the barn. Moody is busy cleaning the lots, feeding the chickens, and milking the cows. "Is the car running pretty good Mister Jim?" "Yes pretty good Moody." "Have you tasted Carrie's wine?" Jim asked Moody. "No sir, not yet. She won't let nobody near dat smokehouse. Carrie been fixing different things all da fall. We should have a big Christmas." "Yes, I hope so," said Jim. For a few minutes, he looks away and thinks about Louise. As he leaves the barn, he looks in the direction of the Agar's Plantation, but that's all. Jim is lonely for Louise and Mildred is lonely for Antone.

After a while Carrie calls out, "Everybody get ready for supper!" Moody rings the bell and everyone gets washed up. The boys put up the nuts they found. At supper they all talk about Christmas. Carrie chuckles because she is real happy. She thinks, "Willie will be in from the North Range soon. It's going to be a hot time now from plantation to plantation."

It always happens like this at Christmas time. After they get through working, Carrie sings, "Nobody knows the trouble I's seen." It's not a very jolly song. But it is to Carrie because she feels jolly as she clears away the table and washes the dishes.

"My, you are happy tonight Carrie," says Genelle. "Yes honey, dis is the time of year dat the savior was born." She gets through and goes out to get the helpers' dishes. During the winter months they put a tent-like covering over their table. It's nice and warm out there in the yard. One of the helpers asked, "When you seen Willie Carrie?" "Not since before Thanksgiving. He will be in off the North

Range for Christmas, and he better have some place to take me."
"We know Carrie, you want him to take you to the preacher man."
"Child, you know something!" They all laugh out loud, "Haw haw
haw!"

The next morning starts the Christmas week. Monday will be
Christmas day. Carrie starts to cook the hardest things first. She
makes a bushel basket of teacakes. She already had the nuts hulled
for them. She puts nuts in her dough. When they are done she
sprinkles sugar on the top of them. Then she gets ready to pack them
away for Christmas. Each day she cooks some more. On Wednesday,
she cooked a wash pot full of chitterlings and put them up in jars so
the smell would be gone by Christmas. On Thursday, she makes
headcheese and puts it in the cellar to keep cool. Of course you can
hear her singing or humming some song the whole time. "My Missie,
we show gon have a big time. Dis food ought to last two weeks."
"Yes we hope so," says Mildred.

Carrie was feeling real good inside. She asked Mildred, "Will your
friend be here? The one you had his picture long time ago." "Oh, oh,
no," Mildred stuttered out. "He won't be here Carrie, and don't ever
mention his picture before Jim." "Oh no Ma'am Missie! I won't. I
feel glad all over today. I hope everybody is happy as I am." "That's
good Carrie," replied Mildred. She was happy because she knew
Willie was going to talk to her about when they would be going to
see the preacher man.

The next day, Carrie cleaned and ironed some. The kids were
outside. She and Mildred talked about Christmas dinner and the
guest list. "Who all will be here Missie?" "Well let's see, the Agars I
guess. Oh Carrie, have you seen Louise anytime lately?" "No Ma'am
Missie, I ain't." Mildred continued, "The people from over the river
will be here." "Oh good Miss Mildred! Dae always brings me a pretty

Christmas present," Carrie said. "Yes Carrie," she replied. "There will be about twelve families here all together." "Yessum I show hope my plum puddings comes out dem cans all right." "Don't worry Carrie, they will." Carrie giggles. "I'm going out to the crick and see about some of my nuts. I put up some for my cooking."

It was a cloudy day today. The fields were brown. Most of the men were busy. Some of them were cutting cordwood. Some were fencing. Some had gone hunting and you could hear the dogs barking. Carrie was looking out across the bare fields thinking of different things, and humming every once in a while. Smoke was making a long streak across the sky. Everyone is getting ready for Christmas. You could almost smell the good smells from across the way.

You could hear the sound of an ax as it cut into some wood. Two of the helpers were cutting stove wood for the stove. They will have to have plenty of wood for all the cooking that will be done for Christmas. Carrie gets through early and goes home. She is going to get some of her best dresses and aprons ready. She won't have much time during the Christmas week to wash, so she washes her things and gets them all ready. She hums, "Way Down Upon the Suwannee River," and "Waiting for the Robert E. Lee." She sews up the holes, puts on buttons, and lets out seems the rest of the night. She goes to bed late. But she is real happy, because Willie will be back soon for Christmas. Not much sleep for Carrie tonight.

On Christmas Eve Carrie gets up early in the morning all full of joy. She starts singing as she goes up the road. The roosters were crowing; the hens were cackling, and the dogs were barking. You could hear the "Moo" of the cows, and the pigs giving out a grunt. Carrie thinks, "They all feel the Christmas spirit too."

Everyone is up in the Nutterlow house this morning. The usual,

"Hello Carrie," is heard all over. Carrie fixes breakfast and cleans the house. There's not too much to do because the house was cleaned long ago. Carrie cooked some more goodies today. The Nutterlow kids decorated all day. They changed everything and made the house look so pretty. Everyone was full of glee, even Mildred didn't feel so sad. She did think about Antone though. She thinks about last year when she and Antone exchanged gifts as early as December fifth. This year, Antone is in France. "How I do miss you Antone," she thinks. Then, she falls right in line with all the different things that have to be done in the house today. She helped the girls wash their hair and roll it up in kid rollers or paper for curls while they all laugh and talk about tomorrow.

Christmas Eve night, there was so much excitement in the Nutterlow house. Jim and the boys had gone to get their haircuts in the village. It was easier now that they had the car. The girls were busy wrapping gifts for their friends that will be there tomorrow. Everyone is just so happy, even Judd the dog is happy lying in front of the fireplace.

The Christmas tree is all trimmed and the house smells of Pine. They have holly and mistletoe all over the house. The smell of pies and cookies is coming from the kitchen. Carrie was still in there cooking. She gets out Mrs. Low's beautiful lace tablecloth. Then, she and Mildred get the dining room table ready. They put a yellow satin undercover on the table. Then they put the lace on top. The yellow satin peeking through the holes of the lace tablecloth is really pretty. The Low girls made a centerpiece of golden leaves; some were yellow like the satin. Mildred had old-fashioned candlesticks with yellow candles. The table napkins were white with yellow borders. The centerpiece had a yellow corn pattern in it too. It was all very lovely. It was all Genelle's idea. She took a homemaking class at school.

She really enjoys making things like this. The other girls helped too.

"Oh, there's Jim and the boys," Mildred said. They came in smelling of cologne. It was the only kind they had back then. It usually came in a glass bottle with a very small neck. Only a few drops come out, but you could smell it almost back to Atlanta. "Hi mamma!" "My you boys smell good." "Yeah, it was Dad's idea," the little Low boy said. "I smell like Carrie's perfume she puts in her cakes." They all laugh.

By now it was getting late. Mildred rushed the younger children in the Nutterlow family off to bed, because Santa was coming tonight. After a while they all were ready for bed. Carrie had already gone home. Everyone tossed and turned in their beds with excitement. Finally, everyone was asleep. Mildred stayed awake for a while thinking of Antone, then she fell asleep. Everyone's dreams were about the gifts and the guests that were coming. The younger children dreamed of what Santa was going to bring them.

At midnight the roosters crowed, and then again around three in the morning. But it's too early yet. When the rooster crowed at five o'clock, the youngest Low boy was awake. "Boy! Get up everybody! Santa Clause has come! Oh boy! Get up!" he said. All the gifts under the tree were marked. The girls were a bit lazy and didn't want to get up yet. But all of the boys were wide-awake. Carrie was already in the kitchen. "Merry Christmas" was heard all over the place.

Every Christmas morning someone blew a cow horn. They all would listen for the echo of the cow horn, then they call out, "Merry Christmas!" The blower blows 3 short blows then a long one to let you know he heard your echo. Christmas is in full force now. The whole family unwrapped their gifts. "Oh thank you," is said as they hug and kiss each other. One of the younger Low children said, "Don't forget to thank Santa Claus." "Yes of course dear. Thank you

Santa Claus," Mildred said as she winked at Jim. He smiled, and winked back at her.

Mildred gave Jim a beautiful jacket with a green satin lining, a pair of spats, and a new pipe made of Chestnut. The man at the store said the pipe came with a box of Prince Albert tobacco. Jim liked to smoke a pipe. He gave Mildred a silk Kimono from Japan he bought from a Chinese peddler, along with some gold earrings, and a pink satin quilt. Jim told Mildred about Miss Jenny. "She's an old negro woman that lives across the river. She pieces quilts together–all kinds of pretty quilts." "Oh Jim, it's beautiful." She hugs Jim lightly. Jim took a lock of her hair in his hand, feels it, and gives it a snatch. Mildred said, "Oh you," and they smile. All the time, Jim wonders how Louise Agar is getting along with his baby she's expecting.

He helps the boys with their toys. They put the trains together and wind them up. They put a boat together too. In those days, almost all of the toys had to be put together and wound up in some kind of way. The boys got toy rifles, and something you stepped on called sonnover gum. It pops all over the place. Carrie said, "Get out of here with dat stuff. My goodness, you gon set my red petticoat on fire." "Awe Carrie," they said. She gets the broom after them. They pop some more and run. Carrie giggles. Then she starts to set the table because the guests will be there around noon. "Oh Miss Mildred, I hope dis is a good dinner." Mildred replied, "Don't worry Carrie, everything will be just fine."

The Low girls get dressed in their best for dinner. Mildred puts on a very pretty green velvet dress with a yellow tie. Carrie is dressed in her printed dress and yellow apron. The men that help around the house had on their new cheap pants, and checkered shirts. They opened their gifts out in the yard. All the boys got red flannel undies from Jim and heavy work clothes. Mildred bought them red and blue handkerchiefs, neck ties, and socks. Some had a Rayon look. The helpers called them silk socks. They were all given gloves, and cigars. They laughed, talked, and opened their gifts. As always there's a jug of Carrie's good wine. "Look at my gift," somebody said. "Look at mine. Hot Dog!" said another. They all let out with a chuckle.

One of the kids came in and yelled, "Here comes company! Mom, Dad, here comes company!" The helpers rush out to help the guests get out of their buggies. Not too many cars were there. Jim was the first one to buy one. Jim and Mildred stand at the door to greet each one with hellos, hugs, and lots of handshakes. They all go into the parlor. "Oh Mildred, your house looks just divine. It always looks good." Mildred blushes and replies, "We had fun decorating it, the girls and I–mostly the girls."

The guests who had children brought them along too. The girls go with the girls in the Low family to their part of the house. All of the boys go outside with the boys in the Low family because they had a lot to show their friends. "Gee, did you make this?" asked one boy. "Oh yeah!" The Nutterlow boys show off their new car. One of the boys had built a doghouse and all kinds of birdhouses. Some weren't even up in the trees yet. One boy built some kind of thing to ride in. The other boys were real excited.

Then they went down to the barn to look at the prize pigs. Some of the sows had new litters of pigs. Later on, they went down to the brook. The Nutterlow boys told them how many brook trout they caught in the summer. They were stretching the truth some, but who would know.

They walked on down through the meadow. But the meadow wasn't a lush green color. It was brown, its winter coat for this time of the year. They went on over across the bayou, then across a field to show the boys where their dad goes hunting for squirrels, and rabbits. One of the boys that was visiting said he would like to come over in the summer, but they always go to Texas in the summer to their dad's other place. "Oh yeah?" one of the Nutterlow boys replied, "I think I'd like that though–maybe." "Yeah, it's o.k. I guess," he replied.

Christmas day was a joy. Carrie served dinner around three. There were two families beside the Nutterlow's, and twenty-four kids including the Nutterlow kids. Carrie was real happy. The plum puddings came out of the cans all right, and the lemon sauce was good, not too sour. Carrie was swift on her feet. She got around and served all the dinner. One of the helper's wives helped with the dishes. She wasn't trained to serve like Carrie was because she only worked in the fields.

By six thirty dinner was over and everyone was so full. There was deer meat, turtle meat, turkey, frog legs, wild prairie chickens, turnip greens and kale cooked together. They also had collard greens and sweet potatoes that were baked until the sugar just busted out of them. They had white potatoes that were whipped until they could float. There was roast pig, baked ham, and an old-fashioned country ham. It was the kind you can smell cooking from miles away. There were pumpkin pies, Carrie's spoon bread, her old-fashioned gingerbread, and she didn't forget to make her famous shortening bread. There was also a pot of chitterlings and Carrie's good biscuits and cornbread made with at least six eggs. There was also rabbit meat, squirrel meat, and some corn. Carrie opened her prize canned fruit too. It was a real feast.

They didn't eat all of this food on this day because there would be more people coming the next day, and the next day, and every day after that for a week. This is the way the big plantation owners celebrated Christmas, and Jim Nutterlow was one of the big ones.

The men showed off their gifts and their new pipes. The talked about how much cotton they ginned, how much corn they made, and how much hay they bailed. They all told a lot of tall jokes too. The ladies talked about their new clothes, their children, all the gossip, the showboat, and how those girls kicked up their legs and showed their underwear. They also played some kind of old card game they played around that time.

After a while the men joined the ladies and they danced The Two Step, The One Step, The Waltz, and The Black Bottom. One of the ladies got full of Carrie's Grape wine and did the, "Shimmy Shake Like My Sister Kate." Her husband took her out for air and slapped her face. She told him, "This is Christmas, and we are having fun." "Alright! Just don't shimmy," he said. They went back in and everyone was waltzing. No one said a word. They stopped for a while later and drank some more of Carrie's wine. They had so many to choose from. There was cherry, blackberry, grape, persimmon, and muscadine wine too. All of them had been aged for this day.

After midnight the company was all gone. Everyone was a little high. Carrie and the girl picked up and cleaned everything. Then Carrie gets the kids into bed. What a day and just think, this was the first one. Carrie and the other girl went home tired but happy. Jim and Mildred must have really had the Christmas spirit. They slept together for the first time in six months or more. Late over in the night Mildred drifted off into her thoughts, "Oh Antone, what are you doing tonight?" Jim drifted off into his thoughts about Louise, wondering how she was and where she was. For the first time since it was built, the Agar's plantation was closed this Christmas. Jim sighs, and falls asleep. By now, Mildred is already asleep. This was a big day. The Christmas holidays went by nicely. Each day different families would come from different plantations miles and miles away.

Soon, it was New Year's Eve. The men were busy outside getting their fireworks ready for midnight. The ladies were sitting in the parlor just talking. One lady asked about Louise Agar. Mildred said, "I don't know. I haven't seen Louise since late summer. She was here to a party one night, but she didn't have much to say. She just looked at everyone right funny. Their plantation is closed this Christmas." "Yes, I noticed it was closed when we passed. I heard she was sick," one lady said. "I heard that too," said another. By the time the men started to show up again, the gossip about Louise ended. They all ate some more of Carrie's good cooking, drank some more of her wines, and some hot rum too. All of this helped them to start telling some more tall jokes again.

The night passed and in nothing flat, it was midnight. The men rushed out and began shooting their fireworks. For miles and miles you could hear the guns shooting, and bells ringing. The plantation helpers beat on tin tubs, buckets, and anything that made a noise. Someone let out with a loud, "Lord Happy New Year," and the echo carries. They do this until one o'clock. The New Year was truly welcomed in.

After a while, the Nutterlow's company started getting ready to leave for home. They all have that one last drink, and bid the Low's good night. What a good time they had in their home. Jim and Mildred stand in the doorway until all of the guests have gone. Jim looked at Mildred, and she looked at him. He takes her in his arms, "Happy New Year Mildred." "Happy New Year Jim." Jim picks her up and swings her around. They laugh and get ready to go to bed.

"Christmas is all over for another year." "Yeah," Jim said. Mildred's thoughts go out to her Antone, "I wonder where you are tonight." She closes her eyes, laid down on the bed with her head on the pillow, and her arm across her face.

Jim just looks at her for a while. Then, he goes to bed.

The next day there wasn't too much going on around the Nutterlow house. Everyone slept late. The helpers didn't have to get up early today. They always looked forward to this day. Later on, everyone was up and around. The Nutterlow's went into the village to see Aunt Maggie. She was all dressed up for them. This used to be a special trip for the Nutterlow kids, but they are growing up now. To the older ones it was a bore, but kids in those days went where their parents said go. They tried to make the best of it; besides, it made Aunt Maggie happy.

On this day, she told them all about the Blue Coats. This time, the Nutterlow's didn't spend the night. Jim had work to do tomorrow, so they left early. Aunt Maggie was real happy. She hugged them all goodbye. She bought presents for everyone. They thanked her and waved goodbye.

Before long, everything got back to normal. The helpers got up early the next morning. There was a fence to fix, hoes to sharpen, and everything else that goes on around a plantation. Some of the men shucked and shelled corn.

By now, Jim Nutterlow had his own Gin Mill. Some of the men grounded the corn for the mill. Some of the men were helping with the cows, others were checking the horse's shoes. One day Jim bought about fifty goats, for what nobody knew. He also bought about fifty head of sheep. The plantation would really go haywire with both of them. Jim decided to leave the sheep, but he brought the goats home. Some of the men from the other plantations were there. They kidded Jim about the goats. Jim really had a large plantation.

Chapter 11

Spring came early in Centerville this year. By March, the helpers had plowed all the land for planting. By mid-May all the fields had been planted. Jim had really put the men through, but he was really proud of his plantation. The weather had been good. Not too much rain, just enough to make the crops pretty. The Spring Fair had started again. This time it was in New Orleans. Jim told Mildred about it. "Oh Jim, I'd like to go with you." "Well you understand its auctions of stock mostly." "I know," she said. "All right Mildred," he replied. Jim went out to the barn to look over the hogs. Mildred started to get her things together. She thinks to herself, "Maybe I'll find out something about my Antone."

They left on Thursday. Jim carried his prize hogs and steers. Moody and Willie went to take care of the hogs and steers. They got into New Orleans Friday morning, and checked into a hotel. Jim gave Mildred some money, kissed her, and left for the fairground. "I'll see you tonight honey. You go shopping. I've got to see about the stock." "Alright Jim," she replied. Mildred cleaned herself, got all dressed up, and went out. She went over to the house where Antone and his mother always stayed when they were in New Orleans.

The maid that worked for Mrs. LaBlanc was there and was glad to see Mildred. Mildred asked her all about Antone. The maid told her someone told Antone's mother that while she was there, "You and Monsieur Antone were together all the time, and you stayed here with him. Madame LaBlanc was very angry. She threatened to disinherit Monsieur Antone. They left right away for France." "Have you heard anyone say they heard from Monsieur Antone?" Mildred asked.

"Oh yes, their agent hears from them all the time. Madame LaBlanc hasn't been too well since returning home from here," she said. Mildred was real happy to hear this. She left and went to downtown New Orleans to shop some. She thinks, "I'll do some more shopping tomorrow."

Jim came back to the hotel at six o'clock. He was all smiles during dinner. One of his steers won the blue ribbon and one of his hogs too. "Oh Jim," Mildred kissed him. They went down on the river to the riverboat and they danced. Jim was really thrilled. He had also heard that Louise and Josh Agar were in Atlanta and Louise had been real sick, but was better now. Jim was happy to get this news. Although they both had their thoughts, Jim and Mildrded danced and acted like two people really in love.

They left the RiverBoat dance about four in the morning and went back to the hotel. Jim was so tired, he just fell asleep. Mildred stood by the window and looked out into the early morning darkness. After a while Mildred gets into bed. Jim stirred some. Mildred just laid back on the pillow and began to think. She thinks about Antone, the gift she gave him last Christmas and the gift he gave to her. Then she thinks about his mother and how she could make her grown son jump when she snaps her finger. She wonders what it is that she has over Antone, and why she won't let him go. Then she thinks of what she heard about him. He was married, but his mother ran the girl off, or paid her off. She heard that she had the marriage annulled.

Mildred thinks of Antone's eyes, his hair, his hairy chest, and how clean he was all the time. She thinks of Jim and how he always smelled like horses. Her last thought was of Josh and Louise Agar. She wondered why the Agar's plantation was closed. She thinks of how much fun Josh was whenever he attended one of her parties.

She also thinks, "Louise looked funny the last time I saw her. And she looked at me funny too." Soon, she drops off to sleep.

Jim stirred again, this time he was awake. He starts to think too. He thinks about all the people that were at the last big party they had, all of the jokes they told, and all of the gifts. Then he thinks about the plantation and all of the livestock. He thinks about the children. "Genelle is a lovely girl. All my kids look alright." He thinks about Louise and how they first started meeting down by the bayou, how sweet she always smelled, and how soft she was.

He thinks about how mad she could get and how he would look into her eyes, snatch her up to him, kiss her, and she would just go limp. Then she would start begging him for a baby. She wanted to have one of his babies. She wanted his body next to hers. He thinks about his last night with her, how soft she was, and how sweet she was. She cried some too that night. She said she wished that night would never end. She begged him to stay. Mildred stirred some. She was restless. Jim was restless too. He just laid there, looked away into the night thinking about Louise. Soon, they both drop off into a deep sleep.

The next day everything was about the same at the plantation. The helpers were busy clearing the land, burning the brushes, spreading fertilizer, and getting ready for spring planting. Jim goes into the village everyday hoping he would hear from Louise. Moody had to drive Jim every day. He was too upset to drive, but his excuse was he wanted Moody to learn to drive real well.

Before long it was spring and all the planting was going on. The helpers were really busy. Jim moved in two more families from over the river. His plantation is getting larger and larger. Carrie no longer has to do the washing. The new woman does the washing. There is so much to do now with the Nutterlow kids getting older.

Carrie sings all the time nowadays. She is real happy because
Willie talks about what they are going to do after they go to the
preacher man.

Big Jim is indeed worried about Louise and he had a good reason
to be. Louise went to Atlanta to have the baby. Josh came in from
Carolina and went directly to the hospital. He got there just in time
to hear Louise say she was sorry, and that the baby was Jim
Nutterlow's baby. She told him how much she loved Jim. Then, she
looked away and died. The doctor told Josh she was just a bit late
and the opening of her womb had never developed. It was the size
of a child's womb. Back then, the doctors weren't taking babies
through cesarean section. Josh just looked past the doctor in shock.
Sometime later, he was finally able to leave the hospital. His sister
was there with him, and they left together. They didn't say anything
to each other. All Josh could think of was Louise saying over and
over again, "Please forgive me Josh. I'm sorry. I'm so sorry."

Then he thinks, "Jim Nutterlow? How could I have been so
blind? How! How!" He thought about how he was gone all the time.
He said to himself, "Sure it was a lot. But it was always business,
never anything else." In the dark, with the lamp out, Josh sat in a
chair in his sister's bedroom. He sat there, looking out the window,
and thinking the same thoughts over and over again. He thinks about
their marriage, how pretty Louise looked, and how happy he was
getting a nice young thing like her. Josh was older than Louise. "But
she said she didn't care," he thought. He dropped off to sleep every
once in a while, sitting in the same chair.

Fortunately, his sister was there to take care of him. She came in,
made him get up and wash himself up. She tried to get him to eat,
but he wouldn't. "Josh, you can't do this at your age," she said. He
finally did get up, but he walked around in a daze.

Three days later they buried Louise and her unborn baby. Josh just stared. That was all he could do. His sister wiped her eyes once or twice. The chapel was full because there were a lot of people from Centerville in Atlanta visiting, and doing different things. By midsummer, the news got around. It seemed like everyone knew except Jim and Mildred.

Josh Agar never came back to his plantation. His sister closed his plantation home and moved all of their beautiful furniture to Atlanta. Louise had good taste and his sister was plain. She kept Louise's dresses hoping maybe they would help her look better. Josh went to Tennessee, then back to the Carolinas. He moved about from place to place. He tried to forget this way.

One day Mildred went to the village. Jim was up at the North Range. Mildred thinks, "He's been up there a lot lately." But because she had more important things to think about, she didn't spend much time trying to figure out why. Instead, she goes on into Uncle Henry's store with the only private phone in town. She had to call New Orleans. When she called, the maid told her Antone had been there but he only stayed a short while. Mildred thinks, "Why didn't Antone call me or try to get in touch with me? Oh Antone, why?" Then she thinks about his mother. "I bet that's why he came alone. I bet she made him hurry back." Mildred goes home early and just weeps about Antone.

Later on, Carrie comes in. "Oh Missy, you crying." "Yes Carrie," she says. "I know honey. You must be lonely with Mr. Jim up at the North Range, and Miss Louise being gone and all. And she was your best friend. I know how it is honey." Mildred just says, "Yes Carrie." Carrie starts to sing, "I couldn't hear nobody pray." Mildred goes to sleep. When she wakes up, Jim is home. "Oh hello darling!" "Hello Mildred." She noticed a change in Jim, but she doesn't say anything.

Chapter 12

Fall came early, and everyone was busy working in the fields. Jim left home early and came home late. One day Mildred asked him why he spent so much time away, but he didn't answer her. The holidays were almost upon everyone again. Genelle was in Texas going to school this year. Her friend went, so Jim Low let her go too. She wrote a letter saying she was now wearing her boyfriend's sweater. She was real happy. Mildred was glad to hear this. She really did act like a real mother. Who knows, Mildred may have loved her children. She really did see that they were well cared for.

After Jim and Mildred talked about the letter they got from Genelle for a while, she and Carrie got their heads together to plan a party. She always had a big party every year. This year was no different. Everyone came, and this time there were more cars. Jim noticed this and started thinking to himself, "Oh Louise, where are you?"

That night he danced every dance, and almost all of them with Mildred. They acted like they had just met. Jim drank so much wine. He was really in the clouds tonight. Everyone was a bit high. They flirted with each other as always. No one said anything about the Agar's until about midnight. Someone said, "Where did Josh Agar move to?" Another one replied, "Atlanta I heard." Jim just looked from one person to the other. Mildred acted real sweet and lady-like.

As they all started to leave, Jim and Mildred stood in the doorway and bided everyone good night. Every once in a while she would look Jim's way and smile. He would try to smile but deep inside she knew something was wrong. Mildred was so sweet. She never said anything.

After all the guests were gone, she threw her arms around him, kissed him, and said, "Oh Jim I love you so much dear." It was an act but Jim was lonely and worried about Louise. Once again, he thought about the days and nights he spent with Louise and how she used to beg him to give her one of his babies. That's what she wanted most of all. Jim closed his eyes, took Mildred in his arms, and said, "Oh Mildred, Mildred." She went limp. He picked her up and took her to the bedroom. She took off her clothes and rolled into bed. But Jim sat there for a while. Soon, Mildred fell asleep. Jim kept sitting on the bed thinking about his children, the plantation, and Carrie. "Carrie!" He gets up and rushes out to the porch. A few minutes later he was gone.

Carrie was still up when Big Jim got there. He just walked in like he was mad. "Oh Mr. Jim!" she said. "Hi Carrie," he replied. Carrie thinks, "He had stopped coming down here." She asked, "Is anything wrong Mr. Jim?" "I don't know Carrie. I just don't know." He sat down on the bed. Carrie sat there and looked at him. He talked for a while, then he left. Carrie went to bed. She was sure glad he left early. Willie was coming later and that would be too much for Carrie.

Jim couldn't sleep that night. He sat up thinking about Louise, how much he loved her, and how they used to meet down by the bayou in the afternoon. He thinks about how sweet she would smell, and how tight everything was to get into. Just about everything goes through his mind, the same thoughts over and over again. Then he thinks, "Where are you Louise? Why are you still in Atlanta? Why Louise, why?"

Jim finally went into the bedroom, took off his clothes, and got into bed. By now it's real late. Mildred stirred some, "Oh Jim." "Yes Mildred," he replied. Mildred snuggles up to Jim. They were real loving for the first time in a long time. Mildred closed her eyes and thought of her Antone. "Oh Antone, how I miss you my love." Jim's thoughts were about Louise, how much he loved her, and how much he missed her. Mildred snuggled up to Jim again. But he let go of her thinking only of Louise. She let go thinking only of her Antone.

Chapter 13

The next day everything was the same as usual. It was a cool January day. Jim told Mildred he was going to Atlanta for a few days. Mildred said, "Oh not to buy more cattle or land I hope." Jim looked away as he said, "I just don't know yet." Mildred said, "Well I'll go as far as New Orleans with you." They got their things together and were ready to leave around midnight. They acted the part well of a happy husband and wife. Mildred got off the train and kissed Jim and told him to hurry back. He just looked at her.

Jim got into Atlanta the next morning and went to a hotel. After a short time, he set out to try and find out something about Louise. In town, he met someone that used to live in Centerville. She was one of those walking gossip sheets. She told him how Josh came in just in time to hear Louise Agar say that the baby was another man's baby. Louise told him that she loved this other man. She asked Josh to forgive her, then she died. Because she had been gone for a long time, the old gossip sheet didn't know who the other man was. But she did tell Jim that the other man was Josh Agar's neighbor, and he lived on the plantation right next to his. Jim's heart skipped a beat. He almost fainted. Luckily, he leaned against the wall of the store they were standing by to steady himself. The lady asked him if he was all right. Jim told her, "Yes, it's the heat." He told her that he had been ill. "You take care of yourself young man," she said as she strutted on down the street.

Somehow, Jim made it back to the hotel. No one will ever know how he suffered. He beat his hands. He beat his head. He just put himself through. He blamed himself, and it didn't help that Josh knew he was the other man. Jim stopped for a minute and thought,

"I better get home!" Quickly, he threw his things in his bag. The next train left at twelve noon, and Jim was on it. All the way home he thinks, "I knew something was wrong. I knew it!" During the train ride home, Jim was quiet. He was deep in thought thinking, "If only I could have been with her." He tightens his fist until they turn red.

Jim got home late that night. Moody met him at the train. He only said, "Hi," and was quiet all the way home. Moody tried to tell him what had been happening around the plantation, but Jim only said, "Yes, Uh huh." "Miss Mildred got in today," said Moody. But Jim didn't say anything. Moody decided to hush. They rode on in silence.

Moody got out, grabbed Mr. Jim's bag, carried it to the porch, and said, "Good night Mr. Jim." Jim just walked on in the house. He left the bag on the porch. Lying in bed, Mildred stirred some. When she opened her eyes, Jim was standing next to the bed. "Oh Jim darling, I didn't know you were home. Did you have a good trip?" Jim said, "Yes," and went limp across the bed. Mildred said, "Oh, darling you must be very tired. I was a little tired, but I'm rested now." She rubbed his temple and in a few minutes, Jim was asleep.

The next day, he slept late. Mildred knew this was strange, but she never said a word. The helpers had already gone to the fields to do their work. Jim was up when Carrie came in to make the bed. "Oh, Mr. Jim!" she said. "That's all right Carrie, I'm getting out." He went into the kitchen for coffee.

Mildred was dressed and as lovely as ever. "How was the trip Jim and what did you do?" she asked. After a while he said, "Looked at some land." "Good grief Jim!" "Don't worry, I didn't buy the land Mildred!" "Alright darling, you don't have to get mad." Jim looked at her and said, "I'm sorry Mildred." He ate some, then he left.

Mildred watches him as he walks out. She notices how different he looks since he got back from Atlanta, even how he walks.

She knows there is something wrong and thinks, "There's something wrong. I can feel it." But she doesn't say anything to Jim. When Carrie comes in she says, "Oh Carrie, don't you think Mr. Jim looks sick?" "Yes Ma'am Missy, he do look sick," she replied. Then they sat down to make plans for dinner.

Jim came in later but not for dinner, he had been to the village. He had a letter from Genelle in his hand. He read the letter to Mildred. "She's coming home? This is only February. Why is she coming home?" Mildred asked. "All I know is what the letter said Mildred!" Jim snapped. "All right Jim!" she replied.

Carrie cleaned Genelle's room and went down in the flower pit to get some flowers. The house was all cleaned for Genelle's home-coming. Everyone was wondering why she was coming home. Word of mouth helped spread the news all around town, and to the other plantations. By the end of February, everyone knew Jim's oldest girl was coming home from school.

It was raining the day Genelle's train arrived, but they all went anyway to meet her at the station. She looked beautiful. She was small like her mother and very pretty. Jim hugged her as she stepped off the train, then Midred said, "Now tell us what's the big secret. Why have you come home?" "Oh mother, I'm getting married!" She had the ring on her finger. It was a solid gold ring. "I had to come home and ask you and daddy." Mildred said, "Well, what about school?" "Oh, I plan to go back. He's going to teach. His family raises cattle and they have money mother. There is nothing to worry about. Daddy what do you say?" "We'll talk about it at home honey." Jim replied. They all got ready to go home. Genelle talked on and on about her beau. By the time they got home, Mildred and Jim had agreed to let her marry her Texas redhead.

Carrie greeted her when they got to the house. "Lawd a mercy

Miss Genelle, I show is glad to see you. Honey child come here."
Genelle rushed into Carrie's arms and hugged her. She was breathless. Then she started to talk about her Texas redhead all over again.
"Now slow down," Mildred said. "When do you and your young
man plan to be married?" "Oh Mother in June of course. I had to
come home to get ready. He will be here for a short stay to meet you
and daddy. His parents are coming too mother. Oh goodness! We
have to get ready!"

After dinner Mildred and Genelle sat down to go over the plans,
the invitations, and all that goes with a large Southern wedding. Big
Jim was a prosperous plantation owner and he had plenty of money.
The wedding was going to be the biggest wedding Centerville had
ever seen. Jim told everyone he met in and around the plantation.
Jim welcomed this news because he was so grieved over Louise's
death.

After everyone was settled and in bed Mildred thinks as she
brushes her hair, "Antone I will be seeing you sometime soon my
darling. You have to tell me why you treated me this way." She tied
up her hair in ribbons and went to bed.

Genelle didn't sleep much. She had to write to her fiancée. She
wrote the letter telling him her mother and father said she could be
married, and they will be looking for him and his parents to come to
Centerville.

The next day, Mildred was busy planning everything in her mind.
Her thoughts about Antone were put aside for now. First, they made
out a list of all of the large plantation owners. Then they made a list
of out of town guests. Each day a name was added. Everyone in the
Nutterlow house was excited and happy. Even Big Jim was back to
normal–somewhat. He was up early overseeing the plantation, and
telling everyone Genelle was getting married.

March came in with a hailstorm. The next day the sun was out. The helpers were busy cleaning up behind the storm because the corn was soon to be planted. After a few days, they started plowing and planting the corn. Jim was real happy. His thoughts of Louise and her death were in the back of his mind, for now. Jim and Mildred talked all the time now. They were just like they were when they first got married.

Jim and Mildred had never discussed their money before. So one day, they went into New Orleans. Jim signed all the necessary papers making Mildred part owner, and giving her half of all his land, money, and cattle. They held hands and strolled down the in-laid brick streets of New Orleans. Mildred thinks about Antone for a moment. Then she said, "Oh Jim, let's eat at Sardie's today." Jim said, "Won't it be too expensive?" "Expensive?" Mildred replied. They both think about their trip to the bank and smile. They walk up the street to Sardie's Motel to have dinner.

Sardie's has the best food and the finest wines. While they ate, Mildred's mind wanders as she thinks of how she and Antone always ate there. Jim said, "Honey we better get going." "Alright darling," she said. They left holding hands. The train left at five, and Jim and Mildred were on it. Mildred was real happy because she had been thinking about the money business. Now it was all settled. She thinks to herself, "How perfect this is for me."

Moody met the train at the station. Mildred bought so many things. Fortunately, Jim and Moody were able to put all of the boxes in the car and they rode away. Mildred hummed some. Jim said, "Are you tired honey?" "No," she replied. Back at the plantation, Carrie and Genelle were up just fussing around the house.

Genelle's fiancé and his family would be there this weekend, and the house was all prettied up for their arrival. Jim bought new saddles for the boy and his father so they could go horseback riding while they were there. Mildred bought fine linen and lace tablecloths, and some new old-fashioned Southern China. Everything was ready.

On Saturday morning, they were all up early to meet the train. Genelle stayed as close to a mirror as she could so she could look her best for Tex. The train came in right on schedule. Tex was the second one off. Genelle rushed to him and they embraced. Then his father and mother stepped off the train. Genelle rushed over to them because Tex had already introduced her to his parents. Tex and his family were real pleased with the warm welcome they received. Genelle was so excited. Mildred was her sweet self, and Jim acted as if he was happy too.

They spent the next few weeks horseback riding and swimming in the lake not too far from the house. By now it's late May and real hot in Centerville. The rest of the Nutterlow kids were coming home from school all excited over the news that Genelle was getting married. Lotis was very happy because she was going to be the maid of honor. Tex's best friend would be there by June. He had to get some things ready first.

Everyone was busy making all kinds of preparations for the wedding. Carrie cooked like never before. It was good that the new family was now living on the plantation. Carrie thinks, "Else I'd never get through." Every day she had to cook a big meal. The Nutterlow's were really doing it up big for Tex's people and they were really taking it all in. Carrie thinks, hums, and sings a little as she cooks.

Every day, friends and neighbors came by to bring gifts and to help Mildred get everything ready. All the furniture had to be moved around out of the way to make room for the guest, and to make a plain view for everyone to see. Jim and Genelle were going to walk down the winding steps to the parlor when the music started to play. The music would be played on an old organ, which was partly hand carved out of the best wood Italy had. Jim bought the organ and had it shipped over when Genelle was seven years old.

All of May plans were being made. Everyone had a nervous stomach and had to drink some of Carrie's bitter apple tea. Jim bought flowers, all the prettiest kind. The house was decorated from the ceiling to the steps outside. All the barns were white washed with white paint. Jim bought a rug and had it cut to fit the walk so when you walked up the brick walk, you walked on the bright red rug. Everything is ready now. Tex's mother had to go to bed for a day. She was so nervous. Carrie thinks, "She not so nervous. She's so full in the corset cause dae sho can eat."

Carrie is real happy these days. She hums and sings a lot. She and Willie have been making all kinds of plans. She knows for sure now, he's gonna take her to see the preacher man real soon. Genelle comes into the kitchen. "Oh Carrie, I'm so happy!" She threw her arms around Carrie and hugs her. A few tears dropped out of her eyes. "I sho is happy too honey child."

Big Jim doesn't know it but another family up on the North Range left last night. They leave late at night now, about four or five families at a time.

Schools were starting to close all over, and the Nutterlow kids are coming home. They too will have to get ready for the wedding. Genelle had to have just everything, so she and Mildred left for New Orleans right away. All day for two days, Genelle tried on dresses. Finally, she decided on the very first one she tried on. Mildred was too tired to travel, so they stayed overnight.

After Genelle was asleep Mildred called the LaBlanc's place. It had been closed. The maid that used to live there with the LaBlanc's had gone to France. Mildred thanked the lady that answered the phone, and hung up. Then she slipped back into the room. Genelle stirred just a bit, but she was still asleep. Lying in the bed in the dark Mildred thinks, "Why did they close the house? It was always kept open." As she falls asleep she thinks, "There's a lot I must find out."

Chapter 14

Mildred and Genelle left for home with all they could carry. Jim met them at the train station, because Moody was busy cleaning and painting the barns. Everything had to be very clean. So Jim helped Mildred and Genelle with the packages and drove them home. Genelle hummed, "I'll Walk You Home Again Kathleen." Jim smiled at her. Mildred laid her head on Jim's shoulder, and they all started humming, "I'll Walk You Home Again Kathleen."

Back at home, Lotis was happy because she was stuck on a picture of Tex's best man, Warren. He arrived the next day. He was very good looking. He wasn't a red head like Tex. His hair was black, and real wavy. He had dark brown eyes too. Lotis went limp when Jim brought him back from the train. He liked her right off too. Everyone was there to greet him except for Patty. She never did come up from the barn. She was down there with Moody.

Even though he was only there for a week, Warren got to enjoy all of the things planned for Tex and his family. He went horseback riding, swimming, and of course he ate all of Carrie's good cooking. Before long, the week was coming to an end. Friday was May 30th, and Saturday was May 31st. No one in the Nutterlow household paid much attention to it being Memorial Day. Big Jim did though. He went to the cemetery for a while. His people were buried there in Centerville.

Saturday night, Mildred had Carrie to serve supper out on the front lawn. The preacher was there, and some of the guests from over the river were there too. That night, everyone pretended to go to bed but no one was sleepy. It took Carrie a while to finish serving and cleaning up after everyone. When she got home, she pulled out her real nice dress up dress, irons it and her real dress up apron too. She was tired, but she wanted everything to be ready for the big day tomorrow.

Finally the big day arrives, June 1, 1924. The sun rose dark pink. There was a pretty blue sky and everything was green. There was a soft breeze, not too strong. Carrie got there just at the peep of day and started making breakfast. Her and the new girl fixed breakfast until the sun was two or three hours high. Soon, everyone was up getting washed and ready for breakfast. While they were eating Mildred had the new girl to fix up the beds and get the house in order. The wedding would be at twelve o'clock noon.

After breakfast, everyone started getting ready, all excited and a bit nervous too. The ladies were sticking hat pins in their heads. By eleven o'clock, everyone was dressed except Patty. Finally, she came out wearing a very beautiful blue dress with her hair and eyes all done up. Everyone gave her a second look. One lady whispered to the other one sitting next to her, "Look, out of all the Nutterlow girls, she's the prettiest." The other one agreed. They were two busy bodies that may or may not have been actually invited to the wedding. Who knows, they may have just showed up.

The signal was given for everyone to get into their proper places. Jim's face began to turn red. Tex's best man kept feeling into his pocket to make sure the rings were there. Tex's mother wore a white dress with a pink orchid. Mildred wore a beautiful gown of white satin and lace. With or without the dress, Mildred was beautiful anyway. Everyone was dressed so lovely. The young single Southern Bells were all dressed in their frilly dresses. Lotis' dress was a lovely light aqua with small rose buds around the waist. The flower girl's dresses were just like Lotis', only their dresses were organdy. Both Tex and his father's suits were made in St. Louis.

The organ player starts to play, "Here Comes The Bride." Everyone's eyes started to stretch because no one has seen Genelle all morning. Then the moment comes. Genelle walks down the long winding stairs on her father's arm. Jim looked and felt ten feet tall. Genelle was his first born. His suit was specially made in Atlanta. Mildred thinks, "He looks as handsome as he did when I first met him." Today they both forgot about their secret lovers and think only of Genelle.

Her dress was a lovely trousseau frock, made of blue cotton lace. She wore matching slippers, and a corsage of white mums. The dress also had pink buds around the waist. She looked so lovely. Jim just looked at her all through the ceremony. Mildred shed a few tears and remembered when she married Jim.

Carrie had the dining room table over laid with an imported linen tablecloth, and a centerpiece made of silver and crystal. It was filled with pink roses. There were all kinds of cakes and plenty of pink lemonade. Of course, there was some of Carrie's famous homemade wines too. This was really the wedding in Centerville. Jim had already made arrangements to have the pictures put in the Atlanta paper. All the way across the river, the wedding was the talk of the town. For the rest of the summer, everyone talked about Big Jim Nutterlow's daughter's wedding.

Genelle and Tex spent their honeymoon down in old San Antonio. They plan to live in Waco and raise cattle. Tex's father had plenty of cattle. Big Jim had plenty of money. He gave them all he could and that was more than enough. He was real happy he could give his first born everything. He thinks, "They'll have a good start." Then he thinks of how his dad gave him a big start when he married Mildred.

Chapter 15

Shortly after the wedding, Mildred started making her plans to go and find Antone. Each day little by little, she packs. Carrie is making plans too. She and Willie are going to the preacher man. One by one the helpers on the plantation were leaving. One day Jim asked Willie about one of the families that lived up on the North Range that he hadn't seen for a while. He rode up there one day, and there was no one there. Willie said, "I really don't know. Maybe somebody got sick or a big tent meeting just got started." Jim never gave this a second thought because they always worked hard and he never had any trouble. He wondered though, but he knew those tent meetings could last at least a month.

One day, he rode past the Agar's Plantation and thought about Louise and how much he loved her. Then he thinks, "I'll tell Mildred the truth." Mildred also plans to tell Jim the truth about Antone. But they both kept waiting for the right time. Planning the wedding kept them busy, and they were alone together very little. But now with the wedding over, they both think that maybe they'll have some time to talk.

One day Jim came home early. Mildred had been to the village. The wedding was still the talk of Centerville. "Oh Jim," said Mildred. "Where were you? I went to the village today." Jim told her he rode up to the North Range. "We got a card from Genelle and Tex." "Oh!" Jim reached for the card. He beamed because she said they were having a marvelous time and she described all the things they were doing. Jim looked at Mildred. She looked at Jim. He walked over to her and she reached for him. Jim took Mildred in his arms and she went limp, "Oh Jim."

For the first time in a long time, they spent a quiet night together. They talked about how they first met and how much they loved each other then. Jim loved Mildred tonight like never before. Little did he know she plans to leave him.

The next morning, they were up early. They were going into the village because by now it's fall and school will start soon. They wanted to see the kids off to school. After the big wedding, and their summer vacation, all the rest of the Nutterlow kids started packing to go off to school in the fall.

The kids were all grown up now. Lotis will get out of school in the spring. She has already applied for a job at a hospital in Atlanta. Terrance plans to join the Marines. Patty hasn't said anything about her plans. Aaron is going to Boston. He plans to be a doctor. After he was so sick that time, he decided he wanted to be a doctor. Bobby had always longed to work on a ship. He always watched the ships when they came into town. He used to say, "One day I'm going to sail one of those ships." So he plans to go away to a school where he can learn how to sail ships.

Jim told Mildred he was real proud of the family she gave him. Mildred felt a bit sick inside thinking of how she hated to be all stuck out when she was pregnant. But after Jim gave her half of the money and property, she was real happy. She walked over to Jim and hugged him. He took her in his arms and kissed her. Then he looked at her and said, "Mildred." But Carrie came in to say that dinner was served. They walked to the dining room locked up arm to arm. Jim was really going to tell her about Louise. He has been trying to tell her for a long time. But they just sat down, ate, and looked at each other real happy like.

After dinner, Jim asked Mildred, "Honey, what are Patty's plans?"

"I don't know. She hasn't said. I plan to ask her soon."

Jim said, "After a while honey, it won't be anyone here but you and me. Our kids are growing up and leaving us." "I hate to think about it," Mildred replied.

Jim still plans to tell Mildred the whole truth, and ask her to forgive him. Mildred plans to go to France after all the kids are gone. She doesn't want to tell Jim until she is well on her way there. She plans to find her Antone. Jim and Mildred both have plans, but they haven't told each other about them yet.

There is a reason why Patty hasn't told anyone about her plans. She has been secretly seeing Moody every chance she gets. She's in love with him, and has been for a long while. She and Moody have kept quiet about everything. Ever so often when the family would go away, Patty would stay home so she could be around Moody. It all started when she was around ten years old. She would wait for Moody to help her down off of a horse, or put her on top of one.

One day when the family was gone, Moody was working in the hog lot. He got through early, cleaned himself up, and put on his nice clean clothes. By this time Patty rode up on her horse and called out, "Moody! Moody! Come help me down." Moody rushed out of the barn and helped her down. She held onto him, looked into his eyes, kissed him, and told him how much she loved him. Moody was a very fair skinned, coffee cream colored man with naturally curly hair. He was very good looking.

He tried once to tell Patty it would never work, but Patty had everything all planned out. Many nights after everyone was asleep, she would slip out the back and go sleep with Moody. She finally made him admit that he loved her too.

Patty didn't go off to school that fall when the rest of the kids left. She stayed at home. Her excuse was she had planned to go away to school or take up Home Economics and Horse Training.

Big Jim was pleased with this. He thought she was planning to do this in Centerville, and that was great. He thought about how she always liked the out-door life. All of the children had a share of money. So Jim decided he would give Patty her share to get her set up for this. He went to New Orleans one day and bought Patty just loads of new clothes, and horse-riding things too. Mildred went with him, and they took out some money at the bank for her. Jim told Mildred, "She's going to be a real horse woman too." Little did Jim know what was really in Patty's mind.

One day, Patty told Jim and Mildred she wanted to go to South America for a while before she settled down. Jim was all for the idea. Mildred said she didn't think it would be good to go that far away from home alone. "Well Daddy, I hope it's alright. I asked the new family that just moved on the plantation if they would help me when I started my work. But they said I should ask you." "Oh honey, of course, of course," Jim said. "I plan to take the man's wife with me so she can fix my meals, wash, and clean for me." Jim felt ten feet tall. His daughter was going on a trip with her own maid. He told her, "All right honey, all right."

Everything is working out just fine for Patty. She is really going to South America to be with Moody. He left a few weeks ago. He told Jim he was going to see a sick brother. Moody had been saving every dime of the money Big Jim paid him for work, so he had plenty of it.

Patty quickly started making plans to leave. One day while she was planning everything out she thinks, "How will I ever get all of these clothes away from here?" But, bit by bit when Jim and Mildred were away, she would take them to the village and ship them to South America. It all worked out just fine, because Moody was already there to receive them. Little by little, she got all of her clothes shipped. Then she took her trunk. She told Jim, "Don't worry

Daddy. It's not much, just a few things." "All right," he said.

By the end of the week, Patty was on a ship sailing to South America. The maid was with her. Her family had already left a few weeks earlier with Moody. They told Jim they were going to see about some sick relatives too–so they said. Because the maid was with her, Big Jim didn't think twice about it. This is just the way Patty had planned it. For days, Patty and the maid laughed and talked about how well everything worked out.

After ten days at sea, they finally arrived. Moody was there to meet the ship when it pulled into the port. Patty and Moody hugged and kissed each other in front of everyone. You see, one night late in October, they went across the state line and got married. Patty put on some dark make-up. The justice of the peace thought they were both colored, just real light skinned. Along with all of this excitement, Patty was expecting a baby too. After they hugged and kissed each other some more, Patty told Moody, "Oh Moody, I love you." Then they left the dock and went home.

Moody bought a large house, and had it done up almost like the one she grew up in. Moody had good taste. Patty said, "Oh darling my favorite color, yellow." Then she kissed him again. Moody had to remember, he didn't have to be afraid anymore to take his wife in his arms and kiss her.

While he kissed her, he thought about how he and Patty used to watch Big Jim take Louise Agar into his arms and kiss her in their secret hideout down by the bayou. One day, Patty was out walking in the woods when she came upon her father and Louise. She's known about them since she was twelve. She took Moody down there to see them lots of times. They never said anything to anyone because they were in love too.

After they were all settled in, the new family that lived on the

North Range, and left the plantation with Moody, bought a small house not too far from where Patty and Moody lived. They were all fast friends. Moody had a job when he got there working with horses for one of those big shot South Americans. There was another boy that worked there, but Moody was the overseer of the place.

Patty waited until after the baby was born to write Big Jim a long letter. The baby was born in April. In May she wrote a letter telling Jim how much she loved him and her mother, and she thanked him for all he had done for her. Towards the end of the letter she told him how she and Moody were married just before they left Centerville, and who married them. She talked about the baby being a month old, how beautiful he was, and how he looked like Big Jim. But he looked like Moody too.

At the very end of the letter she said, "You see Daddy, I've known about you and Louise Agar for years. I knew that her baby was yours. The same love I have for Moody, I feel as if you had the same love for Louise. Give us your blessing Daddy because we truly love each other. Always walk and stand tall. I will always remember you and love you, my daddy Big Jim Nutterlow. Kiss mother for me. Your loving daughter, Mrs. Charles M. Moody."

Jim read the letter over and over again. He got mad and thought, "I'll go get her!" Then he thinks about the baby and the nights she had already spent with Moody. He thought about the men in his family, his dad, his old granddad, and the nights he spent down at Carrie's house. Jim sent her a check for the baby and wished her good luck.

Everything starts to come together now. It all starts to make sense to Big Jim. Moody said he was leaving to go see a sick brother. The new family that had just moved in on the North Range said they were going to see a sick relative too. He wondered why it was taking them so long to get back. And the new boy from up on the North Range, let his wife go with Patty. But they were already in South America waiting for them to arrive.

Chapter 16

By now it was Spring, and Big Jim had plenty of time to think things over. Even though the plantation land was plowed, the helpers started leaving by the dozens. Some left at midnight, others would leave just before day. By summer, all of the helpers were gone. One night shortly after midnight, Willie and Carrie took all of their things over to Lucille's house, loaded up their wagon, and left. He took Carrie to the preacher man just before they left Centerville. This made Carrie very happy, because she and Willie always fussed about going to see the preacher man. Lucille got a letter from them about a month later. They were living in the Flat Lands down south, and they were very happy. They didn't have to slip off to the cotton house or to Lucille's house to see each other. They no longer had to be afraid of Big Jim anymore.

Mildred left after all of the children left. She left Jim a note telling him how she met and fell in love with Antone, and she was going to France to look for him. At the end of the note she wrote, "I know you will forgive me Jim, because I forgive you. I found out about you and Louise Agar during one of the last trips we made together. I got off the train in New Orleans and you went on to Atlanta, remember? One night I ate dinner at the same restaurant Antone and I used to eat all the time–Sardie's. There was an older lady there who was eating alone too, and we started talking. She told me she was born and raised in Baton Rouge. She used to live in Centerville, but she moved away shortly after her husband died.

She said she knew Louise, and the whole Ivy family, even some of their other relatives too. In fact, she seemed to know a little some-thing about some of everybody, or at least those who live in or around the places we have been. Because she is getting older, she moved back to her family's home in Baton Rouge. But she said she still loves to travel, shop, and meet new people.

On the night we met, she had just got back from a trip to Atlanta. While she was there, she found out about Louise. She told me how just before she died, Louise told Josh the baby was by someone else. She didn't know who the man was. But when she said the man lived on the plantation right next door to Josh Agar's, I knew it was you Jim—I knew. While she continued to talk, it all started to make sense to me. Your frequent trips to the North Range, the strange places you would come out from around the plantation, and the way you always had to rush off whenever I wanted to talk. Yes Jim, it all became clear to me—everything."

Towards the end of the letter she wrote, "Try not to be too angry with Patty. She and Moody are very much in love. Anyone who looks at them together can see this. I found out about them by accident. I was restless one night and saw Patty leaving out the house through the back door. Being her mother, naturally I wanted to know where she was going so late at night.

You won't like this Jim, but I found out she was going to be with Moody. The way they kissed each other, I could tell they had been meeting like this for quite some time. I was angry at first. But I thought about how I came to love Antone and why. This must be what you felt for Louise. Am I right Jim? Then I thought about how we met and how much in love we once were. I don't know how or why it happened, but somehow, some way, we lost that Jim. Give my love to the children. And again, try not be too hard on Patty. Unlike your nightly visits to see Carrie, they have been together a long time. And Jim, they really do look like they love each other.

The last time I saw her, she looked just like I did when I was pregnant with Genelle. You see, the first time a woman gets pregnant, the baby always makes her glow. I don't know when their baby is due, if it is a boy, or a girl. But be sure to give them all my love and my blessing too.

In spite of all Jim, we did have a wonderful life and a beautiful family. Although we lost our love for each other along the way, I have always been proud to be the wife of Jim Nutterlow. If it helps you, do what I do now. Always remember the good times we had. They're gone, but they will never be forgotten. With all my love, Mildred." Like the letter he got from Patty, Jim took Mildred's letter and read it over, and over again. Every time he reads it he says to himself, "She knew, she knew."

Mildred did go to France, and she found her lover Antone. He was married to a lovely French girl, and they had three children. His mother gave him all the money under one condition. He had to marry Jeame because Gee Gee liked her. Mildred also found out what his mother had over him all this time. Antone was lazy and didn't want to work. He married the girl so he wouldn't have to work anymore, just see after the money that was left. Antone told Mildred why he did this very cold like. He left, and they never saw each other again.

The last thing anyone heard about Mildred, she was going in and out of every flea bitten joint in Paris drunk, and looking like a hag. She was no longer the pretty Mrs. Jim Nutterlow with all of her frilly dresses and sweet perfume. Those days were long gone. She spent all of the money Jim gave her, and has gone down to nothing. She does anything she can to get a cheap drink. More and more each day, she hates Antone for doing this to her, and every day she wishes she had stayed with Jim. But she feels like she could never go back to him.

Because the paper is starting to tear, Jim took the letter Mildred left him, and the one Patty sent to him from South America, carefully folded them back up, and put them back inside their envelopes. He sits them on top of the mantel in the parlor, because he likes to look at them almost every day. At least once or twice a day, he walks through every room in the house. Sometimes if he is real quiet, he can hear the voices of the children, Mildred, and even Carrie.

It's late Summer now, and Big Jim knows he's all alone. He has his big empty house full of nothing but memories. Every day he gets up and rides over his land. People passing by can see him either sitting on his horse, or standing in the middle of the fields. For hours and hours, he's there looking and thinking about how it used to be. For as far as his eyes can see, there is nothing but acres and acres of plowed ground.

The End

For more information about the author, the editor, upcoming books and events contact us at:

acresofplowedground@gmail.com
godsowninc.org

Reviews can be made wherever the book was purchased.

Made in the USA
Columbia, SC
12 December 2024

47796624R00067